Hypnotherapy for Spiritual Regression
Life between Lives

About the Author

Dr. Michael Newton is a counseling psychologist, master hypnotherapist, and teacher. He has been on the faculty of higher educational institutions and has served as a group therapy director for community mental health centers and spiritual renewal organizations in cooperation with hospitals and social service agencies. Now retired after forty years of private practice, he is considered a pioneer in uncovering the mysteries of our life between lives through the development of his own hypnosis techniques.

He is the author of the best-selling books *Journey of Souls* and *Destiny of Souls* (winner of the most outstanding metaphysical book award of the year at the annual Book Exposition of America in 2001), which have been translated into over twenty-five languages. Dr. Newton received the annual award for the most unique contribution by a hypnotherapist from the National Association of Transpersonal Hypnotherapists. He has been conferred as a Chevalier of Honor by the Order of Constantine for international education.

Dr. Newton is the founder of the Society for Spiritual Regression (now called the Newton Institute for LBL Hypnotherapy), which is an international organization designed for the purpose of training experienced hypnotherapists in the techniques of life between lives regression. He devotes a great deal of time directing this training program, as well as appearing on numerous radio and TV talk shows and public expositions. He has an international reputation as a thought-provoking speaker.

Hypnotherapy for Spiritual Regression
Life between Lives

Michael Newton

Readworthy
New Delhi

Published in India under exclusive arrangement by
Readworthy Publications (P) Ltd.

Regd. Off	Branch
A-18, Mohan Garden	4735/22, Prakash Deep Building,
Near Nawada Metro Station	Ground Floor, Ansari Road, Daryaganj
New Delhi – 110 059-06	New Delhi – 110 002
Phone: 011-2537 1324	Phone: 011-43549197
Fax: +91-11-2537 1323	Fax: +91-11-23243060
Email: info@readworthypub.com	Web: ww.readworthypub.com

Reprinted from
LIFE BETWEEN LIVES: HYPNOTHERAPY FOR SPIRITUAL REGRESSION
Copyright © 2004 Michael Newton, Ph.D.
Published by Llewellyn Publications
Woodbury, MN 55125 USA
www.llewellyn.com

South Asia Edition 2009
For sale in India, Pakistan, Nepal, Burma, Bangladesh, Thailand and Sri Lanka

All rights reserved. Without limiting the rights under copyright reserved above, no part of this publication may be reproduced, utilized, stored in or introduced into a retrieval system, or transmitted, in any form or by any means (electronic, mechanical, photocopying, recording, or otherwise), without the prior written permission of both the copyright owner and the publisher.

Cataloging in Publication Data--DK
Courtesy: D.K. Agencies (P) Ltd. <docinfo@dkagencies.com>
Newton, Michael, 1931-
　　Hypnotherapy for Spiritual regression : Life between Lives / Michael Newton.
　　　p. cm.
　　　Includes index.

　　　ISBN 13: 978-93-80009-05-6　　ISBN 10: 93-80009-05-4

　　1. Spiritualism. 2. Death--Miscellanea. 3. Soul--Miscellanea. 4. Reincarnation--Case studies. 5. Hypnotism--Therapeutic use. I. Title.
DDC 133.90135　　22

Printed at Salasar Imaging Systems, Delhi - 35

Foreword

For the past few years, Dr. Michael Newton has directed the training of professional hypnotherapists in his techniques encompassing the art of life between lives (LBL) spiritual regression. I was very fortunate to be among his first group of trainees who were certified in the detailed methodology of taking clients into their immortal existence as souls. My own background involved training as a traditional psychotherapist and later as a hypnotherapist specializing in Health Psychology.

Ten years ago, I came across Dr. Newton's eloquently written first book, *Journey of Souls*, and later his second book, *Destiny of Souls*, both reporting on the spiritual terrain between our lives that went far beyond past life regression. I felt they were among the most important works ever published in the professional field of Regression Hypnotherapy and, indeed, in all of metaphysical literature. Dr. Newton's contributions are not speculative. His insights are derived from personally facilitating over 7,000 LBL clients into their spiritual life between physical incarnations on Earth. In my own practice, I am amazed by the revelations that my clients experience and the effect these spiritual observations have upon their values, choices, and life patterns in a here-and-now incarnation.

Now that he has retired from active practice, Dr. Newton has written a chronicle detailing the methods he developed in over three decades of spiritual regression practice to insure that the next generation of LBL therapists are properly informed and can expand upon his groundbreaking work. Whether you are a professional counselor skilled in regression hypnotherapy, or are simply interested in expanding your therapeutic work with clients to include the most important aspect of their being—their spirit—this book will be a valuable resource.

And, if you are not a therapist but a person interested in how Dr. Newton was able to achieve the remarkable results described in his books, perhaps with the idea of experiencing a personal LBL regression yourself, you will find *Life Between Lives* a source of valuable perceptions into the methods and thought processes of a pioneer in spiritual discovery. Much more than a technical manual of methodology, this book will stimulate personal reflection about the marvels of a multidimensional creation and of our part in it, both as a soul and as an incarnated human being.

—ARTHUR E. ROFFEY, PH.D. D.D.
PAST VICE PRESIDENT, SOCIETY FOR SPIRITUAL REGRESSION

NOTE: In the summer of 2005, the name Society for Spiritual Regression was changed to The Michael Newton Institute for LBL Hypnotherapy (www.newtoninstitute.org) in honor of Dr. Newton's years of research and methodology development for training hypnosis professionals to be life between lives facilitators. The old web link of www.spiritualregression.org has been retained for referrals to the general public

Contents

Foreword by Dr. Arthur Roffey, Past Vice President of the Society for Spiritual Regression . . .   *v*
Introduction . . .   *xi*

Part One
The Initial Inquiry

1. Addressing Client Belief Systems   3

Part Two
Preparation for Spiritual Regression

2. Personal Demands on the Spiritual Regressionist   9
3. Importance of Training and Experience   11
4. Practicing Life between Lives Hypnosis   14
5. The Intake Interview   17
6. Client Preconceptions   21
7. A Client's Cast of Characters   26
8. Final Instructions to the Client   29

Part Three
Beginning the LBL Hypnosis Session

9. Induction with the LBL Client   33
10. Stages of Hypnosis   35
11. Deepening and Visualization   38
12. Pacing and Voice Usage   42
13. Final Hypnosis Instructions before Regression   44
14. Moving Backward in Time   46
15. Inside the Mother's Womb   49
16. The Transition into a Past Life   52
17. Checking Conscious Interference   57

Part Four
The Mental Gateway Into the Spirit World

18. Past Life Death Scenes — 65
19. Desensitizing Trauma — 66
20. Initial Visualizations of the Soul State — 68
21. Instructions for Soul Departure — 72
22. Phrasing Questions at the Gateway — 74
23. The Unresponsive LBL Client — 79
24. Overcoming Specific Types of Client Blocking — 83
25. Blocking by the Client's Guide — 85
26. Visions of Light and Darkness while Crossing — 92
27. First Contact with Spirits — 95
28. Interaction with Welcoming Spirits — 99
29. Station Stops for the Incoming Soul — 104
30. Orientation with Guides — 107

Part Five
Life Between Lives

31. Returning Clients to Their Soul Group — 117
32. Identification of Soulmates — 120
33. Recognition of Soul Colors — 124
34. Gathering Information on a Soul Group — 127
35. Primary Soulmates — 129
36. The Inner Circle and Missing Soul Companions — 133
37. Soul Energy — 135
38. Examining Character Types in Groups — 138
39. Clients in the Intermediate and Advanced Levels — 143
40. Taking Clients before Their Council — 145
41. Therapeutic Opportunities during Council Visitations — 156
42. Reviewing Past Life Incarnations — 163
43. Surveying Other Spirit World Activities — 169
44. Life and Body Selection — 175

45. Connections between Body and Soul	181
46. Therapeutic Benefits of Spiritual Regression	190

Part Six
Closing the Session

47. Preparation for Embarkation	197
48. Completing the Spiritual Regression	201
49. Awakening the LBL Client	203
50. The Exit Interview	206
51. Conclusions	209
Appendix	*211*
Index	*219*

Dedication

This guidebook of life between lives hypnosis methodology is dedicated to all hypnotherapy practitioners who access the souls of their clients through the use of spiritual regression, and to those who seek enlightenment about their spiritual life

Introduction

This book represents over three decades of personal research and the development of clinical hypnosis techniques helping clients access their soul memories about the afterlife. The means of achieving a superconscious trance state to recall one's immortal existence is a key element of this book. With heightened perception, ordinary people are able to find their own answers to the age-old questions of "Who am I?" "Why am I here?" and "Where do I come from?"

This is primarily a "how to" book designed as a practical step-by-step guide to what I have found to be the most effective procedures for reaching a client's immortal memories about their life in the spirit world. While the book is intended to be a useful methodology text for experienced hypnotherapy professionals, it does contain new case material not printed in my previous books, *Journey of Souls* (1994) and *Destiny of Souls* (2000) by Llewellyn Publications. The additional case material and the questions I use to elicit spiritual visualizations should appeal to readers who enjoyed my other two works. The three books combined represent a trilogy of research information into the afterlife.

It is also my hope that readers will gain a deeper understanding about the process of what I call spiritual regression and be encouraged to embark on a life between lives session themselves with a seasoned professional.

I started my career as a traditional therapist. Eventually, after I began the practice of past life regression, I discovered the methods necessary for directing life between lives regression. As I approached retirement, after conducting thousands of spiritual regression cases, I realized that it was time for me to begin training other professionals in the art of LBL therapy that had proven to be successful over many years.

In 1999, I started working with various professional hypnosis accrediting associations around the country who gave me approval to conduct an LBL workshop lasting a few hours. I soon learned that at least three or four days were required for training others in this difficult work. Then the National Association of Transpersonal Hypnotherapy (NATH) offered to host a conference devoted entirely to LBL methodology if I would co-direct the training.

In September 2001, one week after the terrorist attacks on America, the first world conference for LBL certification training was held in Virginia Beach. It proved to be an auspicious time for a new hypnosis program of spiritual exploration. This intense course consists of some forty hours of workshops, demonstrations, and supervised experiential practice sessions going far beyond the study of past life regression. I owe NATH a debt of gratitude for their foresight and the support they have given me in the development of this LBL conference and those that have followed.

In time, I realized there was a need for an organization whose sole purpose would be the advancement of hypnosis regression into the afterlife. In 2002, I founded the Society for Spiritual Regression with the help of a dedicated group of LBL hypnotherapists. This training organization is composed of certified LBL therapists devoted to advancing the study and practice of regressing clients into the spirit world between their lives on Earth. One of the primary goals of the society is to serve as a referral base for both the domestic and international community. Our website is www.spiritualregression.org.

If you are someone seeking to learn about your own spiritual history, I would urge you to seek recommendations in finding an experienced hypnosis professional with certified LBL training. If such a person is not available in your area, it may be necessary to travel some distance. Believe me, it's worth the effort. It is important to find a qualified LBL hypnosis practitioner with a passion for helping people uncover their soul memories of the afterlife and who will be sensitive to your specific needs.

With spiritual regression, both past life and LBL therapy are combined. Thus, the hypnosis facilitator should be well versed in the field of metaphysics in order to be able to analyze the karmic influences in the client's existence from both a psychological and historical perspective. I also suggest to members of the public that you arrange for a preliminary interview in your search for a skilled hypnotherapist.

While this text is designed to present the foundations of my research into the afterlife in a systematic fashion, it is not my intention that spiritual regressionists conform to a rigid sequence of hypnosis procedures. In fact, I recognize this material may also be useful for those who wish to employ alternative methods to reach the spirit world. I know that each facilitator brings their own ideas, talents, and experience to the practice of LBL therapy. The application of different approaches to the mind can only enhance our knowledge and perspective of our spiritual life.

I will offer advice on certain issues I feel strongly about but, rather than being too theoretical, I have done my best to sustain this information on a practical level and to simplify as much as possible the conceptual framework involving my hypnosis methods with clients. It is my hope that we are at the beginning of what will become a worldwide movement in the twenty-first century for offering a method that provides new spiritual insight into ourselves. The many uses of spiritual regression can help us understand the purpose for our personal existence and make us better for having this knowledge.

Everything that surrounds us,
Everything that we brush past unknowing,
Everything that we touch which is not felt,
Everything that we meet unnoticing
Has on us swift, surprising, and inexplicable effects.

—De Maupassant

Part One
INITIAL INQUIRY

1

Addressing Client Belief Systems

Before entering into the details of hypnosis methodology connected to the practice of spiritual regression, I think it is fitting to consider your approach to questions about the afterlife. As a spiritual regressionist, you will have clients who are in a personal quandary about their beliefs at the time of their first contact with you. How you respond to their respective concerns might well be the determining factor in their making an appointment.

While a large majority of the people who wish you to help them access their soul memories are comfortable with their beliefs, others are conflicted by religious teachings, concerns over the mechanics of hypnosis in reaching their life between lives, or they may have some skepticism about trusting themselves to you in facilitating their mental entry into the spirit world.

I begin my sessions by explaining to the unsettled potential client that it will benefit them to enter their hypnosis regression with an open mind. I might even tell them that regardless of their belief system, their unconscious memories are probably going to reveal a home in the spirit world that will be consistent with the reports from everyone who has undergone spiritual regression. A skeptic could argue that this sort of reassurance is actually preconditioning the subject. Even so, after conducting thousands of life between lives hypnosis sessions, I am comfortable with making this statement to an anxious client.

When considering bias, there is also the fact that my books about the afterlife are already public knowledge. If a potential client raises the possibility of being swayed by having read these books, I explain that during the many years before my research was published I told most clients very little in advance. Either way, you will find it makes no difference. Once a subject mentally enters the spirit world through deep hypnosis, regardless of their ideology or what I have told them in advance, their reports are going to be similar to everyone who went before them.

I have been told by the LBL hypnotherapists I have trained that they have had clients who never heard of me or my books who, without prompting, have also been consistent in their reports of the spirit world. The differences are in the soul activities they see clearly and those that are hazy. No two sessions are exactly the same because each soul has a specific energy pattern for recovering stored immortal memories and their own unique history of existence.

If a potential client has reservations about metaphysical philosophy due to a rigid belief system, this may have created an inner turmoil that you must address at the outset. This person has contacted you because they do want spiritual information about their higher self and yet ideological reservations are holding them back. I often find in such cases that underneath this mental conflict lies unhappiness and dissatisfaction over how these individuals consciously view the world and their lives. Such people have contacted you because they have finally reached a point where they are willing to seek answers by a new approach. In these circumstances, an eclectic therapist can be a good sounding board for open-ended philosophical discussions that are reflective, interpretive, and encouraging to the potential client.

For example, in America, with our prevalent Christian society, you might be told, "I want to experience what Heaven is like, but I worry that I might be committing a sin by coming to see you." Another slant on this same question could be, "I think there is an afterlife, but must one believe in reincarnation in order to be a candidate for spiritual regression?" I have had clients from cultures where there are strong convictions about life being deterministic, giving them little control over their destiny. Other societies are open- minded about reincarnation and fate but their rituals involve the existence of angry gods, evil spirits, and undesirable astral regions after death. Some belief systems do not allow for a soul-ego that exists in a spirit world between lives. Atheists and agnostics, of course, find it hard to accept a higher power and a grand design in the universe. As I mentioned, regardless of ideological preconceptions in their conscious minds, once these people are in a superconscious trance state they will have the same soul memories about their life between lives as all your other clients.

Thoughtful people with diverse belief systems will contact you because they are searching for meaning in their lives. They are looking for a different sort of spirituality that is consistent and makes sense to them. Once we separate out the extremists and their radical doctrines, all religions have wonderful creeds of compassion, charity, and love. Yet they are also anchored by centuries of institutional dogma that does not appeal to modern thinking. In my view, the world's great religions are too impersonal for many people. In a sense these powerful religions have lost much of the essence of individual spiritual contact with the divine which gave rise to their origins. People are disturbed by this evolution.

The historian Arnold Toynbee stated that throughout the history of humankind when a belief system outlives its attraction as a spiritual model for people it is modified or discarded. We live in a world that is perceived as chaotic. There are those who believe this is of our own making, while others blame the Source that created us and turn away from all faith. Over my years of private practice, I have seen an increase in the number of people who are seeking a new spiritual awareness that is individual and unique to them without intermediaries who wish to impose their will on what they deem is spiritual.

All of us have a tendency to be intolerant of people who don't think as we do. For the spiritual regressionist, having bias toward your own truths is natural but this should not cloud your receptiveness to ideasexpressed by clients. As a life between lives therapist, you want to assist the client in reaching both understanding and equanimity about their existence without imposing your values. Everything the client needs to know is inside their mind. Whenever possible you must allow them to first recognize and then interpret their own memories. Your understanding and positive healing energy is vital as you work to expose the client's inner vision of their soul life. In this way you also facilitate alignment of the subject's vibrational soul energy to the rhythms of their human brains.

I try to explain to my clients, who represent many philosophical belief systems, that we live in an imperfect world in order to appreciate perfection. We strive for improvement through free will and change. Searching for inner wisdom is essential because unless we find a personal inner knowledge beyond those institutional doctrines developed by others long ago, we cannot truly be wise about how to live our lives today on Earth.

Current truths are succeeded by higher truths in each generation, and it is this progression of knowledge and acute awareness of ourselves that is at the core of expressing our personal identity. As spiritual regressionists utilizing the power of hypnosis, we are now blessed with a new medium of therapeutic intervention. If you are able to assist people in seeing the light of divinity within themselves and foster self-discovery, then you will have made a real contribution toward the ultimate enlightenment of our race.

… Part Two
PREPARATION FOR SPIRITUAL REGRESSION

2

Personal Demands on the Spiritual Regressionist

At one of my workshops, I was discussing the effort required in taking people to their life between lives. At the first break a hypnotherapist came up to me and said, "Thank you very much for your time, but I'm leaving. I now realize this work is just too difficult. I have a nice, regulated practice. The hypnosis management requirements of spiritual regression is just not an area of therapy I feel equipped to handle." I told this honest person it was a good thing he recognized these concerns now rather than later.

There is no question that three to four hours of intense work, juggling many balls at once, without rest, is demanding. Essentially, you must contend with the simultaneous interaction of a client's immortal soul and the mental processes of their current human brain. These two egos may be conflicted by disrupted integration. An LBL facilitator must cope with this duality of the client's mind while refining and adjusting long phases of spiritual imagery to support a comfortable passage. To do this you must constantly track their mental journey through the geography of the spirit world. This is called mapping.

The motivations, fears, self-image, and expectations of your client will be determined by the physical, emotional, and mental makeup of their host body. These elements of temperament are influenced by what I call "the I signs of the soul": insight, intuition, and imagination. While your hypnosis subject is telling you about their spiritual life, they are communicating this information through their current mortal body. This can be both confusing and gut-wrenching for them. As the drama of the afterlife unfolds in the mind of the client, their transpersonal view of the other side is affected by how well they can face truths about their real self.

In addition to everything else, you will also be required to concentrate on the many previous karmic experiences your client has had in other bodies so they will comprehend patterns of cause and effect that affect their life today. Practicing LBL therapy will increase your past life regression skills greatly as you move from life to life using the spirit world as a bridge. You may be required to alternate both permissive and authoritarian hypnosis techniques while shifting back and forth between the client's past lives, soul experiences, and current life. Much depends upon their receptivity, which may vary from past life to spirit world settings.

Your task as a spiritual regressionist is to help the client manage their visualizations by allowing them to bring all this information into focus so that they can see relationships by truly understanding their soul and purpose in life and thus be empowered by their session. As an LBL facilitator, this effort can be arduous and requires both skill and tenacity. Certainly we don't engage in personal attachments, but it is a cold therapist who does not feel compassion and empathy for a client who may be going through a difficult time recounting all the reasons why they are in their current body and what their guides and masters have to tell them. No motivated, caring hypnotherapist can remain detached in this work. After a demanding spiritual regression session I usually find myself drained. Clearing my head with hard exercise in the mountains helps me a great deal.

3

Importance of Training and Experience

My LBL training classes have a mixture of licensed therapists and certified hypnosis professionals. Typically, a substantial number of hours in basic and advanced hypnotherapy training is required, along with a few years of private practice. Having some background in past life experience is of great benefit before tackling the demanding work of a spiritual regressionist. One does not need to be licensed as a psychologist, psychotherapist, or counselor to be a skilled hypnosis facilitator. However, when working with troubled clients, some background in counseling guidance is invaluable.

Ethically, therapists are expected to recognize their level of competence and professional qualifications and not employ treatment procedures that are beyond the scope of their training. To all practitioners of spiritual regression who assist clients in seeking the truth about themselves, I would say the more exposure to academic training and professional experience, the better.

The issue of self-awareness is important to you as an LBL therapist since it directly relates to your influence on the client. Your energy is affected by your own intuition, motivation, and integrity. I have great respect for Taoist philosophy. The Taoists believe that inspiration occurs when one's conscious mind gets out of the way of their natural unconscious energy. In a sense, our cosmic chi (energy) is what brings harmony and clarity to the body. Having a keen internal focus also makes you a better therapist.

The best regressionists have a perception that allows them to know something without the use of conscious reasoning. These therapists sense things at appropriate moments when working with people. During LBL therapy it is possible for both facilitator and subject to receive help from their respective guides, and these moments should be recognized, especially in the behavioral areas of making choices and problem solving.

I believe it is possible to train yourself to recognize and analyze symbols which illustrate spirit-world experiences that cannot be defined in a material way. These metaphors may be symbolic of something on Earth that has applications to a visualized spirit-world event. Frankly, there are times during a session when I feel I am somewhat telepathic. This can be a hindrance when I don't consciously block what I am thinking at critical moments with a client who can pick up my thoughts.

I find daily meditation and controlled breathing to be helpful in my LBL practice. In yoga, prana refers to the life force or energy that is manifested in each of us through our breath. As a spiritual regressionist, I manipulate my breathing at times during a session in an attempt to extend my mind into a higher state of consciousness. I may even enter into a self-induced light trance state to be more open to the spiritual forces I feel around me.

Please understand that prana is not the breath itself nor the oxygen involved with breathing but the energy connected to the breath. It is a connection to the energy of all living things as a universal life force. I have worked to train myself to seek the energy pathways necessary to reach a particular client's mind while asking for help from my guide and my subject's guide. I begin by opening my mind and asking for guidance. In this way I try to receive information and not send it. What I do send to my clients are messages of confidence and reassurance.

The key to being a good therapist is to listen. Another is allowing your client to first interpret their own metaphoric symbols based upon what they are experiencing before you engage in your own interpretations. There is a delicate balance between listening and questioning. To know when to speak and when to be quiet is not easy to teach students. In LBL work one must learn when to gently assist a client in understanding a visualization after they have spent time analyzing what they are seeing themselves. This comes with training and practice, and along the way this exercise and your own creativity may enable you to become more intuitive.

4

Practicing Life between Lives Hypnosis

Since the publication of my books, many hypnosis practitioners have contacted me about spiritual regression. There is the impression that if they are somewhat acquainted with past life regression, it is a simple next step to engage in life between lives work. This is not true.

The fact is that most past life regressionists merely jump their subjects from one former life to the next. Some still believe the time between lives is a grayish limbo of no consequence. This notion is changing and I have wondered if it didn't originate with the ancient Tibetan Book of the Dead, where people read that "the time between reincarnations in the Bardo is a maximum of seven weeks."

In the introduction section of my books I explain that it took me a long time to learn the pathways of progression into the spirit world that seemed natural to most clients. After my first life between lives client opened the door, I needed a large body of cases mapping the spirit world before I felt comfortable with the process I use today. Still, after thousands of cases, I realize I have only scratched the surface of our spiritual realm.

Every new LBL therapist finds their own style. You will learn what works best for you to effect a smooth transition from the subconscious mind into the spiritual house of the superconscious to reach the immortal memories of each soul. How you incorporate your new LBL skills into your practice is something everyone must experiment with for themselves.

I have received calls from around the country from past life regressionists who ask, "What am I doing wrong? Why can't I get my clients into a life between lives state?" My first question is, "How long are your client sessions?" "Oh, you know," they respond, "the usual forty-five minutes to one hour." Without going into methodology, I tell them this is part of their problem. To work with LBL therapy you need to reserve a three- to four-hour block of time. Some then remark, "How do you expect me to keep up my client load seeing one or two people per day?"

I try to be polite in explaining that perhaps they should not consider working in spiritual regression unless they are willing to set aside one or two days per week for this therapy. This might be good advice for anyone to avoid burn-out. However, as I tell my students, I must admit that I did not follow this recommendation years ago when I became obsessed with the power of this work and was compelled to only take LBL cases. Some people I have trained are following my example as LBL specialists and I hope their energy levels hold up. Frankly, the work is so tiring I think it would be foolish to see more than one LBL client per day.

What about the number of sessions per client? Before I began training others, clients would come from all over the world to see me and I could only give them one day. There is a much better way. In the years before I was swamped by requests for sessions from the general public, I had an LBL client for three sessions, each building on the one before:

A. I began with the intake interview and a light, half-hour hypnosis session to determine receptivity. If I was unhappy with the level of trance, they came for more practice sessions.

B. Typically, the second session was devoted to taking the client down into childhood, their mother's womb, and the most immediate last life, but with no death scene or entry to the spirit world.

C.   The final long LBL session where I first took the client rapidly to the end of the life we reviewed at the prior session. After a death scene we entered the spirit world in order to maintain continuity of their visions as a soul. I try never to break up this spiritual portion of a subject's recall into more than one segment.

If you engage in the practice of spiritual regression, your clients are going to want tape recordings of their sessions. I recommend the use of two tape recorders in case one breaks down during the session. Also, you have a backup should something happen to your client's master tape. High-quality microphones are essential because people in hypnosis often talk softly.

You may elect to start taping right after induction, at the point where your client begins recalling their past life, or immediately after the death scene. I like to begin taping right after the death scene because then I can summarize this abbreviated past life so the entire tape will be devoted to the client's soul-life.

5

The Intake Interview

At the time of your first meeting with the client it is imperative to establish their goals and your objectives for a solid afterlife experience. The most effective sessions are those where your client knows in advance the step-by-step procedure you will use. This takes nothing away from the mystery and awe of the LBL experience. I explain that our association will be a partnership where the two of us are going to take a journey together into the spirit world.

Of course, you will want to review their background history, especially any former hypnosis experience. As LBL specialists, most of your spiritual regressions will be with people from out of town. If the client states their prior hypnosis exposure was less than expected, or unsatisfactory in any way, you should ask them to explain the circumstances. If they have any inhibitions about hypnosis, you must address this right away or risk the element of self-sabotage. I routinely suggest to new clients who live far away from me and have never been in hypnosis before that they visit a hypnosis person in their area for one short session, just to see if they are capable of achieving a trance state. This saves time and money for all concerned. Some will want to come anyway and that's fine.

Quite a number of clients who come to me with prior hypnosis experience say, "When I had hypnosis before I don't think I was really asleep." No one had bothered to tell these people they were not supposed to be asleep, otherwise they would have been unable to respond to questions. It seems so basic, yet they were not told of the difference between an altered state of consciousness in trance and actual Delta sleep. I explain to the client each of the natural stages of hypnosis and how deep I will take them. This is particularly relevant with life between lives hypnosis, which will be a new experience in trance depth—even for those who have been in hypnosis before.

I want my clients to understand something of the mechanical process of hypnosis without overloading them with clinical details. Too much technical information about trance depth tends to preoccupy some clients about where they should be during the early stages of the session. On the other hand, I want the client to be aware before we start why we will be spending a great deal of time doing physical relaxation and visualization exercises in order to prepare for the proper trance depth in spiritual regression. Basically, I confine my discussions on altered states to the following:

1. The Beta state is a full awake conscious state.
2. Alpha states involve light, medium, and deeper trance levels.
   a. The lighter stages are typically those we use for meditation.
   b. The medium stages are generally associated with recovering childhood memories and past trauma. This stage is useful for behavior modification, such as quitting smoking or gaining/losing weight.
   c. The deeper Alpha states involve past life recovery.
3. The Theta state is as deep as we get before losing consciousness, and it uncovers the area of the superconscious mind that reveals our spiritual life between lives activity.
4. The Delta state is our final deep sleep state.

I summarize this information by telling the client that all these stages involve a natural process of sleep we go through every night, which is then reversed the next morning. I don't complicate matters by explaining that these stages may actually be working simultaneously with one another in different parts of the brain to facilitate verbal responses. Also, I would recommend you avoid expounding on brain wave fluctuations, although it is interesting to note that with the unconscious mind, the deeper Alpha and Theta waves involve larger, more open fluctuations of energy that appear to expose our soul memories.

I try to present a simplified version of altered trance states in the form of light conversation to relieve any anxiety the client may have about hypnosis being "unnatural" or "mysterious." Indirect suggestions in the form of storytelling are helpful. I know there are hypnotherapists who wish to keep the trance process mysterious for effect. However, as I have said, I want the LBL client to feel this is a cooperative effort. If they become actively involved and accept that they have control over the trance depth needed for LBL work, you will elicit greater engagement from them in the long phases of deepening.

With spiritual regression it is especially valuable during intake that you establish a high degree of trust with your client while they are learning about how you conceptualize their soul journey. While you are observing their place on the road of life, they are analyzing your knowledge, confidence, sensitivity, and perceptiveness. Even if they have had past life regression before, what they experience with life between lives hypnosis will be much more intense because it involves their immortality.

At the intake interview, I want to soften any anxieties the client may have over what they will discover about themselves. I explain how many people have gone before them who were empowered by the results. I don't want the subject to dwell on the possibility they might experience some highly emotional scenes. There will be moments in every session when your client will hit some emotional roadblocks.

Some of these will occur in the discovery stages of who they really are, the mistakes they have made, and their level of development. While people can become discouraged at these moments, over the entire session the experience becomes more and more enlightening to them. They realize fallibility is part of growth.

Your clients will see the serenity of their existence in the spirit world as they become aware of the compassion, forgiveness, and love all around them. This experience is so comforting and uplifting that when you give your subject post-hypnotic suggestions, they will consciously remember these beautiful visions of the spirit world, and they will leave your office with renewed hope for their current life.

During intake, I explain to the client that I am going to be taking them back home in a very relaxing way. While mentally connected to the afterlife they are temporarily released from the turmoil of our material world. This is why some subjects actually resist coming out of hypnosis at the end of spiritual regression. I tell the client that going into the spirit world will be like watching a movie about themselves. When we enter a darkened movie theater where we don't know the plot of the story it seems as if the frames of each scene move more slowly. Later in the movie, when we are more familiar with what is going on, everything will appear to be moving faster, as if a projectionist is speeding up the film. This is because subjects soon become part of the scenes and are caught up with the action.

The discussions you have with your client before the actual LBL session begins are meaningful because you want them to be as comfortable as possible about the process. Keep in mind that the mechanical success of hypnosis itself does not depend on whether a subject is highly motivated or especially willing. Despite the intensity of their desire, a less susceptible person to hypnosis will not do as well in reaching a deep trance state as the highly responsive subject.

6

Client Preconceptions

I have discussed client preconceptions pertaining to ideology under client belief systems in Part One. There are, however, other influences you ought to address that could inhibit your client from entering a session with an open mind. The time to do this is during intake. Often, the new client will tell you they have been to psychics, astrologers, healers, mediums, channelers, and other metaphysical practitioners who have told them about their state of advancement, place in the spirit world, soulmates, guides, and many other things relating to spiritual matters.

I try never to denigrate sources of knowledge out of my own area of proficiency, yet clients can be biased by prior information about themselves, which they often find to be inaccurate once they are in a superconscious state. Just as with hypnosis, some spiritual practitioners are very good, while others are less so. The client will know the difference when they see the spirit world with their own mind. I have mentioned that new clients may also have preconceived spiritual bias from reading my books. Here is a typical example:

> Dr. Newton, you are going to find that I am a Level VI blue light. I know (or I have been told) that I am very close to being an ascended master because this is my last life on Earth.

Of course, you must deal with these pronouncements respectfully. Frankly, I find such statements to be just wishful thinking with clients who are in for a rude dose of humility. On the other hand, I have also had clients tell me that from reading my books they feel they are rank beginners. This modest self-assessment may be completely untrue as well. I must also watch my own preconceptions. I remember Harriet, a truck stop waitress from a desert crossroads town near Death Valley, California. She arrived at my office in an old, battered car and wore a frumpy, wrinkled plaid dress. I was taken unawares by her casual, unpretentious manner until she gave me a hug. Her internal energy practically lifted me off my feet. Later, I found that she was one of the most highly advanced souls I had ever encountered.

Harriet was a hybrid soul whose first physical incarnations were on a desert world long ago. The beings there practiced exchanging personalities through some sort of mental transference into the minds of one another. At her truck stop she provided coffee, conversation, and comfort to tired, discouraged cross-country drivers in the middle of the night. I found Harriet had actually come to help in my spiritual quest after listening to me on a national evening radio show.

Conversely, I fondly remember the case of Andy, the boy of great expectations. Some critics of hypnosis regression argue that people come to sessions with preconceived ideas and, once in a trance state, construct scenes of elaborate fantasy to support their own belief system. Andy's case is one example that refutes this specious argument.

Andy was sent to me by his very perceptive mother as a twenty-first birthday present in the days before I stopped seeing clients this young. A tall, well-built boy wearing shorts and flip-flop sandals, Andy entered my office with a breezy confidence that bordered on cockiness. "Hi Doc, I'm ready—let's get started," he said loudly. As I discussed the format for the hypnotic procedures we would use, including his most recent past life, Andy's impatience grew. He told me he was very popular in school and fully expected his last life to be one where he wielded a powerful influence over large groups of people.

At the point in our session where I told Andy to enter the most significant scene in his past life, his face became clouded. Squirming in his chair, he spoke to me in a low, almost ominous tone of voice.

Andy: Oh, no!

Dr. N: Explain to me what you are seeing.

Andy: Oh, God—NO! Hell, no—this is not me—it's not true... I—NO WAY THIS IS ME! I won't accept this at all . . .

Dr. N: Try to relax and just go with the scene without analyzing too much right now. We can move along as rapidly as you wish.

Andy: (resigned) It is me . . .

Dr. N: Who are you? Let's start with what you look like and then tell me where we are.

Andy: (chagrined) I'm . . . a black hobo walking along a railroad track . . . jeez, I'm so dirty . . . hungry . . . my name is Otis . . . I have a torn, faded flannel shirt, old ripped leather shoes, filthy brown coat and pants . . . I'm coughing a lot.

Further questioning revealed Otis was a poor sharecropper in rural Georgia in 1934 who was to die that night at age forty-five. Once in the spirit world, we learned that Andy had experienced many lives where he was arrogant and abusive to people. As Otis he was given a life of unpretentiousness. At the end of his session, Andy and I had a sobering talk about his current attitudes and lack of tolerance toward others that related to old behavior patterns.

I am careful with the sensibilities of my clients. It is not my place to refute what they want to believe before their sessions; I prefer to let self-discovery take its course. Clients will experience scenes in their minds that they may want to resist at first. Besides the advantages of allowing the visualized setting to unfold naturally, I want clients to assume their personal guide is assisting them in uncovering what they need to know. This can be painful, as we saw with Andy's attempts to dissociate himself from Otis.

Periodically, a client will ask during intake, "What if I make things up during my session?" I begin by explaining that to construct a fantasy about the spirit world while in deep hypnosis would be highly unlikely, since hypnosis subjects in a deep trance state are very honest and quite literal about what they see and feel. I then appeal to the practical side of the client and ask, "What purpose would it serve to make up stories after coming a long distance to see me and paying a fee? In effect, you would be cheating yourself." Finally, I will touch on the idea that truth emanating from stored memories of the unconscious mind is bolstered by the ability to reason and think from a conscious mind that is still active. Questioning by a facilitator stimulates the client's power to reason, since both the conscious and unconscious minds are engaged. A word of caution—while the individual personality of every facilitator is reflected in their approach to LBL hypnotherapy, we must be especially careful not to project our own metaphysical belief system into the minds of clients.

During the session itself, clients may be overwhelmed by the information about their spiritual life that is coming to them from the superconscious state. Some clients will say, "Do you think I am making all this up?" There are many ways to respond to this question. I will first ask, "What do you think?" Then I usually continue with the following inquiry: "Do you trust yourself to be totally open with me about the scenes you are seeing and feeling, knowing this would be to your benefit?" With a client who questions a particular scene I might say, "Ask your guide (or council, or soulmates) about your right to accept your own information relating to what you are being told." At the end of an

LBL session most clients will remark that they have a "knowing" that their visualizations are real.

As you prepare each client for spiritual regression, it is imperative that you not make specific promises about what they are going to see in the session. You don't know what is in the client's mind, nor how well they are going to retrieve and accept their memories. I explain this to every client in advance. Most people tell me a single LBL session was one of the most profound mental experiences of their lives. Even so, once in a while you will have a client express dissatisfaction because they did not find what they wanted, or their life did not change for the better after they left you. There are unhappy people in this world who expect hypnosis facilitators to somehow magically produce information that is either not in their minds or is being blocked. Essentially, this sort of person wants you to fix what is wrong in the lives they lead without taking much personal responsibility.

There are people who will show up at your office that are very anxious, or have a disconnected mind set while others come for a lark. Prior notions take many psychological forms with spiritual exposure. Clients can be so overwhelmed by inner-life concepts that they become confused and don't grasp the whole LBL experience. In the end, it is not your task to try and persuade someone filled with self-doubt of anything. They simply require your support and more time for reflection.

7

A Client's Cast of Characters

While conducting my initial interview, I review the letters my client has sent me about their life and goals and have them bring me up to date. I especially want to know why they wish to be taken into their life between lives. When I began my research, I assumed the primary motivation for most people would be to learn about their guides, spirit groups, and what they do as souls between lives. All this data is meaningful, but the basic reason most people want spiritual regression is for purpose. They want to know why they are here and what they are supposed to accomplish.

In addressing the issue of purpose, one avenue of investigation is reviewing the most significant people in the client's life. These individuals all have some purposeful role to play which may not be fully revealed until they are identified in the spirit world. I ask the new client to bring a typed sheet of paper with the names and a few words about each person. Then, I record all relatives and non-relatives in chronological order as to when they appeared in the client's life, which I use as a ready reference later in the session.

Part of my appointment notification sheet to a new client reads as follows:

> To assist me in your soul group work during our session, it would be a good idea to bring along a typed sheet listing the first names and relationships to you of people who have impacted

your life. These would include: parents, grandparents, aunts, uncles, brothers, sisters, spouses, children, lovers, and best friends. The list should be as condensed as possible, with only the most significant people. Also, include a few words about their personality. Example: Bill—best friend, humorous, spiritual, nonjudgmental, adventurous.

While I am reviewing this cast of characters with the client before the session begins, I often use another metaphor similar to my analogies of being in a movie theater. I explain that their cast of characters have been given stage roles in the great play of life, and that these actors and actresses are the supporting players for the client's major role. The cast of characters list is my program to the play while I sit in the front row of the theater watching the action unfold.

I tell the client they don't need this reference sheet of players, I do. If they see someone important during the session who is not on the list, it won't matter because significant people will appear regardless of whom the client thinks should be on or off the sheet. For instance, if my client, Jane, mentally approaches her spirit group and suddenly exclaims, "Oh, it's Jim who is coming toward me!", I have only to glance at my sheet to know that this soul was Jane's first love in high school. By the same token, I don't need to know about Aunt Millie in Jane's life if that person had no real impact on her.

While I am on the subject of significant people in a client's life, there is another consideration here that relates to your policy with new clients. On occasion, you will be asked, "My husband (wife, sibling, or friend) wants to sit in on my LBL session. Is that all right?" I would advise that you never allow attendance by other parties, for a number of reasons. Primarily, it inhibits the session, as I learned early on in my practice. During spiritual regression the conscious mind is aware there is a third person in the room.

Privacy consists of the client's right to disclose or conceal. The hypnosis subject must be free of the burden of scrutiny by other parties during the intimacy of spiritual regression because they grow more conflicted when people they know are watching and listening to their innermost thoughts. This is especially true when spouses are present. Confidentiality must be safeguarded. After a session many clients will tell you—even those who wanted to bring someone—"I'm so glad I was alone today. I will share certain information but I won't play my tape for anyone."

8

Final Instructions to the Client

After learning something about my client's background, their motivations for coming, and those people who have influenced them throughout their life, the time has come to give them a general idea of how we are going to proceed to the gateway of the spirit world. First, I explain that while they will enter hypnosis rather quickly, it is the deepening that is the secret to success. I explain in advance that we will do some warm-up exercises together, such as breathing, body relaxation, and visualizations.

Since long visualizations are so beneficial in LBL work, I will cover this subject more thoroughly under Part Three on Deepening and Visualization. However, before hypnosis begins, I particularly want the left brain client to understand in advance that while we are engaging in this activity, no analytical interpretations on their part will be required. I hope to place their penchant for control on hold to increase capabilities for release. With all subjects, I establish beforehand their preferences for certain scenes they might like to visualize. It is my intention to establish trust, and give them the impression they are in control. The subject will be more receptive if there is nothing unforeseen before I have them in the proper stage of hypnosis.

While I strive for spontaneity by not revealing too much about my LBL procedures, I also don't want the client to be disturbed by surprises. Therefore, I tell people in advance that spiritual regression involves moving backward through time and that we will engage in a series of mental warm-up exercises, as if we are preparing to run a marathon together. I explain that after our imagery, or creative dreaming exercises, I will take them down into their childhood. It is vital they understand this transition will be nonthreatening. While the client is in a fully conscious state I want them to know that we are not here to uncover childhood trauma, adding that this sort of therapy is best handled by a mental health professional on a long-term basis. To allay any possible fears about uncovering physical or emotional abuse in childhood, I will further explain that we are only going to talk about simple, happy memories, such as toys, pets, and facts concerning their houses. My methods here are outlined further in Part Three, Moving Backward in Time.

I complete my review of the initial process of spiritual regression by telling the client that after a few stops in their childhood we will then move down into their mother's womb (see Part Three, Inside the Mother's Womb). I point out that while this may seem like a big jump it will be a very easy transition because they are young children when we execute this regression. Then I explain we will spend a few minutes inside their mother, where I will ask some basic questions, before rapidly taking them into a past life.

Actually, queries about the womb may evolve into revelations of the soul joining with the brain, but these details are not something I would preempt by discussing them with the client in advance. I clarify the fact with every client that I am aware they have not come to a life between lives specialist for past life regression. I want them to recognize this past review is necessary but will be abbreviated since our primary aim is to move quickly through a death experience in order to enter the spirit world naturally. When all intake procedures are completed, my desire is to reinforce a cooperative attitude with the LBL client about what lies ahead for them.

Part Three
BEGINNING THE LBL HYPNOSIS SESSION

9

Induction with the LBL Client

I won't spend much time reviewing induction since practitioners new to LBL already have considerable experience in this area of basic hypnosis. However, I shall make a couple of observations about induction as it relates to spiritual regression.

Normally, your choice of a fast or slow induction and the use of an authoritarian or permissive approach depends upon your evaluation of the client's receptivity. Typically, rapid inductions work well with compliant, suggestible subjects; clients who are so hyper they can't relax and require a quick release; and people who have been in hypnosis a number of times before seeing you. The slow, permissive induction works well with inflexible, analytical people who are on guard against being controlled, and also those subjects who react well to a more gentle approach.

I mention the general principles of induction and applicability to hypnosis clients because I want to make the point that I recommend a slow, regulated induction for all spiritual regressions. This approach blends well with prolonged deepening techniques. While the upper Alpha stages work well for past life regression, typically the deeper Theta state is required for life between lives work. Certainly, the pace of induction and deepening is a personal decision, but the reason I give this advice is that in LBL work each stage of hypnosis should be carefully monitored.

However, I have another reason for moving slowly. It is my desire to create an ethereal scene in my office to enhance a transcendental mood within my client's conscious mind. Such inducements as briefly having a soft background of celestial music and using a candle flame for eye fixation allow for a spiritual connection to light and sound. I have had subjects tell me later that the golden flame in a darkened room represented a beacon to the spirit world for them. I encourage this perception while giving my hypnosis instructions and pyramiding the effects of progressive body relaxation exercises. It is here where the subject will become accustomed to the pitch and cadence of your voice as well, which I'll discuss later.

10

Stages of Hypnosis

I have already given the new client a light overview of the Beta, Alpha, Theta, and Delta levels of consciousness during intake. For LBL therapists, I would like to reinforce the conventional belief in our profession that in the Beta state the small fluctuations of brain wave energy are tight and compact because they are suppressed by the conscious mind. In Alpha and Theta these waves involve larger, more open fluctuations of energy. I believe the larger waves expose deep-seated memories without conscious interference. At the same time, the newly exposed information from these larger waves is integrated into the conscious mind, perhaps because part of the brain stays in the Beta state during hypnosis.

When I am asked for a more visual description of the storage areas for soul memories, I use a simple diagram to illustrate the stages of moving through the conscious, subconscious, and finally into the superconscious mind. Imagine the mind as having three concentric circles within each other, from large to small. The three rings are not rigid divisions separate from one another, although they look this way on paper. I see them more as porous layers in a filtering system of human thought. Visualize a stone thrown into water with waves moving outward from the center.

The first, outer layer represents the conscious mind, our critical, analytical, coping, everyday reasoning center. The second, middle layer is the subconscious mind, where all our physical memories, including past lives, are stored. It is also the center for emotion and imagination. Creative, right-brained people seem to be able to tap into this area more easily than those who are left-brain dominant. Deep within the center core of these concentric rings lies the superconscious mind, which houses our divine soul memories.

Utilizing hypnosis stages gives us the capability to pass in and out and between these mental levels that link our conscious, immortal, and divine memories. Our eternal soul-mind has evolved from an energy source of superior conceptual thought far beyond what we can imagine. The superconscious mind reveals our immortal character and its long history. Thus within the Theta state we gain perspective about our origins, all our past lives, the life between lives, and the beings who have helped us advance. The experience is sublime.

The LBL hypnotherapist, moving subjects carefully through deeper stages of hypnosis, will find that some people require more deepening at certain levels than others. You cannot get ahead of your subject or fall too far behind. There is no set formula for client receptivity. Certain people will need to be deeper than others to acquire information about their past lives and the spirit world. The subtle effects of different stages of hypnosis vary between subjects.

The wonderful aspect about this field is that with your help, most subjects seem able to find their own trance level necessary to access past life and LBL memories. It is like they have a built-in range finder. Each subject has their own mental attunement within depth levels. We do have statistics that broadly indicate hypnosis receptivity. National surveys tell us that about 10 to 15 percent of the population are highly receptive, while 70 to 80 percent fall into the moderately responsive range. Thus, 10 to 15 percent are either un-responsive or minimally responsive to hypnosis and, of the clients in this group who are eventually successful, most will require some form of continual deepening right up to the gate of the spirit world.

However, once in deep hypnosis, the success of a subject's spiritual recall does not seem to depend upon their initial receptivity to hypnosis or the speed at which they attain certain depths within various stages of hypnosis. There are more reliable indicators for a good spiritual regression session. If we can assume that depth of trance is associated with the degree of disengagement from one's external environment, subjects who are at a level that suits them are going to be more engaged with their internal visions. They will have a more direct focus when responding to questions. This is highly desirable for concentration.

If the subject appears to be free-associating, or displaying vagueness in their responses indicating too much of a conscious connection, the depth of trance is usually the cause. My LBL students, who are already professional hypnotherapists before they enter spiritual regression training, ask this question: "If revivification produces more engagement in past life regression, does this also hold true for life between lives regression?" I tell them not particularly, and explain why. Revivification means reliving a past event, rather than observing. When a subject is absorbed in active participation with a former body, all five senses are fully engaged in memory recall.

I find that reexperiencing an existence in the spirit world does not require revivification for better results because we are in a non-physical soul state. Certainly, being in a somnambulistic deep Theta state can enhance disclosure all by itself. Even so, I do not find an observing mind, which is one characteristic of a lighter stage of hypnosis, to be restrictive in receiving information about the spirit world. In my judgement, subjects in a superconscious soul state are both mentally observing and participating. Still, spiritual regressionists need to pay close attention to trance depth.

11

Deepening and Visualization

As with induction, there are many fine hypnosis texts covering methods of deepening that I will not detail here except where applicability to spiritual regression is concerned. With LBL clients I employ long, guided imagery. Therefore, I don't deepen using the fractionation method of wakening and reinduction, nor pyramiding suggestions to create disorientation and sensory overload through misdirection. Rather than engaging in confusion techniques against defensive reactions, I will issue some challenges through body motor movement exercises and work with progressive relaxation.

During periods within these stages of deepening, I will attempt to foster an out-of-body experience by the client in preparation for what lies ahead in their soul-state. Since an immortal soul character is always part of your subject's psyche, regardless of the depth of hypnosis, I will employ such statements as: "As an immortal being of pure light intelligence, allow your human consciousness to flow into this light which is the real you."

I may spend up to forty-five minutes in deepening exercises involving long visualizations of beautiful mountain or beach scenes. The use of detailed imagery to alter the cognitive dimensions of experience and heighten emotional attachment is also performed in a progressive fashion. What I am seeking is the subject's total absorption into enchanting scenes where they see themselves moving toward a goal in the same manner that I later want them to experience with their spiritual journey home. I use

Deepening and Visualization | 39

pathways, stairways, escalators, sinking down into warm sand, soft grass, or pools of water, and always I have them floating to prepare them for the soul-state. These progressive visualizations are also auditory and kinesthetic, and are intended to both deepen and prepare the subject for what lies ahead.

Thus, aside from deepening, my visualizations are intended to be symbolic in an Ericksonian sense since they are designed to facilitate passage into the ethereal realm of the spirit world. While I have been exposed to Ericksonian training, I do feel more formal, authoritarian hypnosis techniques are effective in LBL work. Nevertheless, I do utilize a metaphoric, permissive approach to visualization. I attempt to integrate my stories with the personality, interests, attitudes, and emotional levels of my subjects to convey meaningful messages. While I don't always succeed, my desire is to have descriptions fit LBL goals of safety, peace, and healing through the use of both direct and indirect suggestions with guided imagery. Here are two condensed examples:

> Now, I want you to see yourself moving out and away from this room, higher and higher into the distance, toward a range of mountains. Feel the soft, warm currents of air around you as you float past fleecy, white clouds on a quiet, calm day. You feel weightless as you float and drift closer and closer to the mountains as you are carried forward without effort. Soon you pass the first range and drop down lower and lower, where you can see a beautiful meadow in a valley below you. (pause) Lower, lower, and now you see that the meadow is completely surrounded by very tall, majestic trees. The meadow is a completely protected sanctuary. As you reach ground level and approach the meadow, you begin to float around the outside

of this perfect circle of trees while you seek to find a single pathway through which you can pass through the circle to reach the center of this serene, magical place.

I will go on with this story, working with finding the pathway as if an unseen power is directing my client. After this passage into the meadow (representing entry into the spirit world), I will introduce other symbols, such as the golden rays of the sun forming a protective shield of warm light from high above (security), and mention the bright colors and fragrance of flowers and singing birds (enchantment).

I may decide to place the client into a beach scene with endless miles of warm sand (unchanging tranquility), sea gulls wheeling overhead (freedom), and the white foam (purity) of rolling ocean waves (comforting sounds). If the client is comfortable with water, I could introduce a fresh water pool into a scene (cleansing). The use of time in a scene denotes infinity. The following is a short excerpt of this sort of visualization:

> Feel yourself detaching more and more as you float downward, being able to breath easily because it is as if you are floating through time and space with no effort. You feel gentle, warm currents around you, gently caressing your body, as you drift down, down, seeing bubbles of translucent white roundness floating past as they rise higher and higher away from you as you drop lower and lower. Soon you are completely immersed from the top of your head to the bottom of your feet, with your own inner illumination as you move through the water and out into the void of space and time. Time flows as a river passing us as we move through it . . . sometimes with the flow . . . sometimes across the flow . . . not resisting the flow . . . but rather

just letting yourself go as you drift aimlessly, without care or concern, going to that special place where you need to be as if in a dream.

While extensive deepening techniques are an important factor in LBL therapy, I want to emphasize that the length of a three- to four- hour session creates a high degree of disengagement. The subject's mind becomes more dissociated from the body with an increase in linear time distortion. If you have conducted a shorter session or two with your client before actual spiritual regression, so much the better, but this does not mean you should rush visualization sequences in the longer LBL session to save time.

During the spiritual regression phase you will want to proceed slowly from scene to scene before reaching the client's past life death segment. During all this time you may see the need to keep deepening. Combining counting with breathing is also very effective. Preparation for the transition into a past life is an example:

Become more aware of your slow breaths. Each breath is taking you deeper. As I count from ten down to one, take a breath with each count and feel yourself moving further away with each number, closer and closer toward the tunnel of time waiting for you.

I have mentioned how a subject's own mental compass within their higher spiritual self can assist them in reaching the depth they require for specific soul memories. Also, that one must always be aware of the two different magnetic energy fields which are activated between the minds of client and facilitator working together. I bring this concept up again to remind spiritual regressionists that the voice is another means of reaching through the subject's energy field and is useful in both removing emotional blocks and deepening.

12

Pacing and Voice Usage

I try to match the vibrational resonance of my voice to the subject's voice tones to reflect their mood, to connect and assist them in entering the appropriate trance state. Your voice pitch and cadence begins with induction and continues as a powerful instrument of sound throughout the entire LBL session, providing both rhythm and momentum for the client. Carefully pacing a session and using different voice inflections involving the application of sharp, soft, encouraging, and calming techniques takes on greater hypnotic importance during a long mental journey.

While you may not be fully aware of what a subject is experiencing at any given moment in spiritual regression, you want to convey the fact that you are always engaged and interested in what is going on with their processing. I work to pitch my vibrational voice tones to match both the sound and type of responses coming from my LBL subject. This begins with my first instructions to the client and is accelerated during deepening. Refinements in tone may be necessary as the session progresses and the reactions of the subject change. Before the arrival of my clients, I take a few minutes to exercise my voice range and sustain certain notes, especially in the lower registers. Calibrating my voice with that of the client from time to time fosters the merging of vibrational energy.

Sound manipulation to synchronize with the ideas you are conveying is particularly useful with visual imagery. I think it helps with making images more identifiable and meaningful to the client. While scenes are unfolding in the subject's mind, a facilitator must try to keep pace with the subject's visual and emotional transitions from scene to scene. As your LBL subject is both connecting and integrating spiritual scenes, they may move quickly, at a moderate rate, or very slowly. I think it is desirable to match their tempo and volume with your own. It is best to be patient and wait until the subject has completely responded to a question before moving on to the next one.

13

Final Hypnosis Instructions before Regression

After considerable deepening through a long visualization, I give the LBL client the following series of instructions:

> I want you to trust your ability to look at the pictures you will see of yourself in different times and places and feel the emotions connected with these scenes and report back to me anything I wish to know without censorship. I will be your guide in our travels together and others whom you have known and loved will join us, including your own personal guide, who will come to help me to help you and provide comfort and strength.
>
> In the beginning, just look at the scenes and tell me what you can with total confidence. As we progress, your memory will get better and better. You will see more, accept more, and have greater understanding about what you see and feel so that soon you will be able to help me evaluate what you see and feel.
>
> And as you reexperience the feelings and emotions connected with earlier times in other bodies and all you have been before, you will begin to feel a positive release from any mental

burdens from the past. All your memories will be placed in proper perspective and integrated into your life today to bring you into perfect harmony with yourself.

Now, before we move on, I want you to visualize that I am placing a powerful, translucent golden shield of light all around you, from head to toe, protecting you from all outside forces and giving you warmth, radiance, light, and power. Should any negative memories of the past come to you, they will bounce harmlessly off your shield of protective light.

Of course, there are many variations to these instructions and I am sure you will develop protective mechanisms for LBL clients that suit your own style. For instance, there is another command at this juncture you might consider. A three- to four-hour LBL session is going to involve long conversations between you and your subject. Talking is not always easy for some clients when their trance state is deep. There are clients who have difficulty maintaining their level of hypnosis when made to talk extensively. My suggestion would be to state the following with all clients:

You will be able to talk to me freely about anything without awakening. In fact, the long conversations we will have together will only serve to maintain and enhance your trance depth. During our time together you will hear my voice clearly and you will be able to talk to me clearly. Our private discussions will comfort you and assist in your disengagement with the outside world.

14

Moving Backward in Time

One reason for starting with a client's childhood is to expedite easier memory warm-ups in preparation for more difficult recall later. Every therapist develops their own format. I begin by having the subject visualize a long, curving, golden stairway in the sky where each step represents a year of their life. You must check the age of your client beforehand. My instructions are as follows:

> We are going to go backward in time, year by year, to your childhood to look only at happy memories. Your mind holds the memories of everything that you have ever experienced at the age that memory was recorded. You carry all these memories with you now in your more knowledgeable, comprehensive adult mind.
>
> As we descend this stairway back in time to your childhood, you will find yourself going deeper and further back with each count. It will be like I am turning the pages of an old photo album where you will see yourself getting younger and younger and then smaller and smaller as you move further and further downward. Anytime I stop on any step you will be the age you were then.

If I sense the client is not as deep as they ought to be at this juncture, I may also give them an additional exercise involving counting:

> As I count from five down to one, we will approach the top step of this long stairway while you continue to disengage more and more from your body. Five . . . now detaching from your physical body more and more in a safe, relaxing way. Deeper and deeper. Four . . . transcending into the deep mental realms of your mind . . . three . . . letting go now . . . floating . . . floating . . . toward the top step . . . two . . . feeling the lightness . . . as you drift and float . . . floating free . . . now very close to the top step . . . one.

Before I begin counting backwards from the client's current age down the stairway of their life, I usually ask for an ideomotor signal such as:

> Raise the fingers of your right hand when you are ready to leave the top step safely and begin your descent with me downward and backward in time.

If there is any hesitation, I may then turn the stairway into a rapidly moving escalator where the subject will see themselves carried downward without the effort of taking steps.

While counting backwards down the stairway I often skip numbers and rapidly go to age twenty, where I will slow down considerably. I might then stop at age twelve and suggest they float from the stairway to the front yard of the house (or apartment) where they lived at this age. I ask clients to describe the size and color of their house and if they see any tall trees to the left, right, or behind where they are standing. Moving into the house, I take a familiar room, like their bedroom, and ask about the position of the furniture, such as the bed and dresser in relation to the doorway. We look inside their clothes closet and I question them about their favorite garment to wear for school or play. Transporting them back to the stairway to reach age seven we then float forward to their house again (often another house) where I will only inquire about pets or toys.

This first exercise of memory recall is focused on the client learning to identify objects and their physical position in relation to these objects as well as seeing themselves changing in appearance with age. While preparing the subject for the type of spatial visualizations we will soon encounter from past life and spiritual memories, I am checking trance depth as well. For instance, if I ask a client at age twelve to identify her favorite piece of jewelry and she says, "Let me think—I can't remember if I had something I liked to wear," then I know they are using their conscious memory to try and recall past information rather than an unconscious memory where they are actually reporting from the scene and giving me a rapid response.

I will address conscious interference and client unresponsiveness in other sections as we proceed further. Right now you should be aware that an inability to answer questions appropriately in a stage of childhood recall may be the first clear sign of a lack of proper trance depth, regardless of prior hypnosis testing and performance up to this moment.

If all goes well, I then regress the client back to their earliest memory as a child and finally into the womb of their mother at the time just before their birth. I assure the subject this is an easy transition because they are now very young (two or three years of age) when we make this mental descent into the womb.

15

Inside the Mother's Womb

There are clients who will have only vague recollections about being a baby in their mother's womb. This lack of awareness has little to do with trance depth. With these people, I only spend a few minutes asking if their arms, legs, and head are reasonably comfortable, and what they hear and feel. "Can you hear your mother's heartbeat?" is one example. If the subject is unable to respond extensively in a fetal state I don't push them because they may be a rather young or undeveloped soul.

Feedback from inside the womb is my initial contact with the soul of a client and the first inkling I have about the particular stage of development of that soul. There is a great difference between one person explaining to me about how they are trying to calm an anxious mother and what they are thinking regarding the challenges of the life to come and another whose only response is that they are in a dark limbo state, doing nothing and thinking of nothing before their birth.

If I have an experienced soul, I turn my attention to a series of detailed questions involving soul integration with the brain. I make careful notes here, which I expect to use later in the more therapeutic portions of the session. The following are questions I have developed in these cases that appeal directly to the soul-mind of the subject:

1. At what month did you first join the fetus?
2. What was your initial impression of the brain you now occupy?

3. Was it difficult or easy for you to trace the pathways of the electrical circuitry of this brain?
4. What is distinctive about this brain?
5. What have you learned about how the emotional system of this body affects the brain?
6. Overall, how did this body accept your soul integration and was it difficult or easy?
7. How does this body compare with others you have occupied?
8. Does your soul-mind feel this body is a good match or not and why?
9. Why did you choose this body?

I only ask the last question if I am receiving specific answers to my other inquiries, otherwise I will discuss the issue of body selection expectations later in the session. Near the end of the LBL session, when the client is looking at their adult current body for the first time in the life selection room, you may want to refer back to their responses from the womb to gain further insight.

Often you will find there are inhibiting factors for soul integration in the mother's womb. Besides a resistant body-mind or—as some clients say—a heavy, dense mind, there is a second factor that is restrictive to the soul during the fetal stage of life. The mother's mind may be closed down to her baby, either from emotional or physical trauma involving anxiety, fear, depression, anger, or simply not wanting the child. These negative factors may be evident with the first child of a very young mother, especially if she isn't married. There could be feelings of displeasure over being pregnant with an unwanted child late in life. If the mother is in a loveless marriage this, too, may cause her to mentally shut down.

Of course, the more experienced souls can override a great deal of emotional negativity from the mother (and later the world, for that matter) by the use of their refined energy fields. As a spiritual regressionist, it is expedient to inquire in advance about the early family dynamics of clients. This data may assist you in looking for both positive and negative aspects of energy integration between the soul and brain that began within the womb.

I have listed examples of client reports from the womb in Destiny of Souls. For the purposes of this book, I offer another case sampling to demonstrate the quality of information a facilitator can obtain from certain clients. This report is an excerpt from the case of Nancy, whom I consider to be an artist of soul integration:

> Before entering the fetus I usually observe the mother's body between the third to sixth month. I allow my energy to filter in by stages to touch her mind first and then the baby's mind. I do this to harmonize my vibrations with both minds. This is how I prepare for a smooth integration. In my current life, my mother was anxious and emotionally distraught about me as her first child so I sent out energy into her stomach and chest to loosen up the hardened energy patterns I perceived in these areas. It seemed to help. When I join with any child I begin by focusing more on the chemistry and electrical impulses from its brain.

Nancy told me the match in her current body was a good one and the mind was not sluggish, so I asked if she had ever joined with sluggish minds in past lives and what she thought of these bodies. Here was her response:

> Sure, I have had sluggish brains in the past. In these lives my soul needed to be more dominant, where I could impress myself easily on that sort of mind. In such cases the game is to build strength, capabilities, and influence within a sluggish child. On the other hand, the challenge for a soul with a child who has a quick mind is to stay focused with all the impulses and thoughts of this baby and yet still remain flexible.

16

The Transition into a Past Life

There are significant reasons for taking an LBL client from their mother's womb into a past life before entering the gate to the spirit world. The most profound justification for this is the need for a person to experience a death scene in order to cross over naturally. My students ask, "Must the life be the client's most immediate past life?" My answer is no but I would prefer to use the most immediate past life whenever possible, primarily because the end of that life was the last time the client entered the spirit world. Their memories are inclined to be more fresh.

Another reason I like to use the most immediate past life is for its usual relevance to the client's current life. There could be direct karmic issues affecting your client today, such as a negative former body imprint. Going to the source of a troublesome imprint would permit you to desensitize the physical and emotional residue. Although it is true you could do this later in the spirit world, a direct intervention during the actual reliving of this immediate past life would cause reframing to be more effective.

Despite your intentions to enter the spirit world through the immediate past life, your client may override this suggestion and take you to an earlier life of more significance. While not common, it can happen. I have already told the client before starting hypnosis that moving through a past life is part of my sequence plan for their spiritual regression. Typically, I do not dwell on all the reasons why, unless the client raises an objection.

Once in a while a client might say to you, "Look, I can get past life regression at home (or "I have had past life regression before"). I came to you because you are a life between lives specialist, so why can't you just take me from my mother's womb directly into the spirit world to save time?"

For some hypnotherapists I know it will be a temptation to try and take people directly into the spirit world without going through a past life, especially if your client has asked you to do so. I have experimented with this approach and I urge you not to do it due to the following drawbacks:

A. Moving backward from a current life directly into the spirit world may cause confusion and disorientation in the mind of your average client. This is because they have arrived at the back of the spiritual house, so to speak, rather than through the front door. Our souls enter the spirit world from a death experience and anything else is unnatural. While it is true that I could mentally return the client to the front gate, this awkward procedure takes time as well. After all, the past life experience will be an abbreviated one in LBL hypnosis.

B. By rushing them directly into the spirit world, your client will miss all the beauty of what it is like to rise out of a body and cross over naturally into a celestial realm. They may arrive rather lost, with no one to meet them. They will not discover what stations are usual stopovers, or how they normally rejoin their spirit groups. From former death scenes we learn how the individual soul usually enters the sprit world. Is it fast or slow? Do they typically hang around their death scene for a while to reach out to loved ones? Is their first contact with a guide or soulmates?

C. Finally, reviewing a former life allows for more memory warm-up with the client before taking the big step of total immersion into the superconscious mind. A client who has not had past life regression before may be slow in responding to questions about what they see and feel, and so exposure to a past life experience in LBL hypnosis allows them to become more familiar with the process. Thus, they are more responsive to questions upon entering the spirit world.

The question could be asked, "Isn't it just as abrupt for the client to be taken from the fetus into a past life as it is going directly into the spirit world from the womb?" My answer is that there is a difference here because with a transfer from the fetus to a past life you are taking this being from one physical incarnation into another, with most clients not yet in a superconcious soul-state. Consider also that involvement in a physical death scene gives subjects more time to adjust to being souls as they float out and hover over their bodies as opposed to immediate entry into the spirit world from the womb. While a choice between these two techniques may not be as much of an issue with really advanced souls, they do not make up the majority of your clientele.

The moment I begin to take the client from their mother's womb to a past life, I have them visualize a long tunnel that will transport them into their most immediate past life (or a life of greater significance, if they prefer). They are going to be transported from the darkness of the womb into a time tunnel of darkness. These are my instructions:

> I want you to imagine we are now moving into a long tunnel, which will take you into your most immediate past life. This time tunnel looks rather like a railroad tunnel but is much smoother and cleaner. Visualize a perfectly rounded cylinder with an entry and exit. As we now move into the large, round entry, you will notice that everything is black around us. As I count rapidly from ten down to one, you will see the curved walls getting gray and then, at the count of five, very white. Then you will see a huge, round, bright opening at the other end, which we will pass through at the count of one

into a significant scene in your past life. You don't know what that is now, but the moment I count one you will be in another time and place in another body—but you will know it is you.

If I am dealing with a sentient subject who does not produce visual imagery well, I will concentrate on touch, feeling, and emotion connected with passing through a dark tunnel. If there are difficulties here with a hesitant client, once again (as with the stairway, childhood, and womb scenes), I may request ideomotor finger signals, such as:

Raise the fingers of your right hand if you are ready to move with me at this moment through the tunnel of time. Raise the fingers of your left hand if you wish to wait until I start my count to begin this fascinating experience.

Since I am going to initiate counting almost immediately, these two narrow choices allow little time for resistance.

The last of my tunnel instructions are as follows:

Ten . . . out of the womb, into the dark tunnel . . . and now we are picking up speed . . . nine . . . faster and faster . . . eight . . . notice the walls are turning grayish . . . seven . . . six . . . five . . . the walls are now white . . . and you can see a huge, round, white opening in front of us, which will take you into an important past life scene . . . four . . . three . . . two . . . one! We now are outside the tunnel!

For purposes of this textbook, I want to concentrate on the methodology of life between lives rather than past lives. Therefore, I will only briefly describe my next series of questions once the client is mentally into their past life.

1. Tell me first if it is day or night?
2. Is it hot or cold?
3. Are you outside or inside?
4. Are you in a city, smaller town, or the countryside?

5. Are you alone or with someone?
6. How are you dressed?
7. Are you male or female?
8. Are you a small, medium, or large person?
9. What are you doing right now?

Because of your instructions, most clients will take you to a significant scene in the life you or they have chosen, which is usually their most immediate past life. You must be prepared for some emotional event from this scene to unfold. Often it is a death scene. You will want to learn their name, age, and family circumstances, as well as the date and geographic location, if possible, and the events leading up to this scene.

I then inquire about people of consequence in this life. If the subject is responding well, with enhanced imagery and a high degree of involvement, I might also ask who are the major characters from the past life in their life today. Successful responses here do not depend on the advancement of the soul but rather on the hypnosis level of engagement. Thus, with some clients, this question must wait until they are in the spirit world. I try not to spend more than fifteen to thirty minutes in this past life because I want to take them to their death experience as rapidly as possible.

From the opening scene (unless it is a death scene), I might move the subject forward in increments of five or ten years for updates. At the appropriate moment I will then say:

> All right, now I want us to move to the last day
> of your life on the count of three—one, two,
> three! Describe what is happening.

If they are dying of old age, I question them about their surroundings, if someone is in attendance, and how they feel. With more traumatic scenes of death, I will take them through the scene very quickly.

17

Checking Conscious Interference

When I discussed taking the client down into their childhood earlier in the session, I stated that you must check to see if the subject actually feels and thinks they are the young person they once were, rather than consciously straining to remember earlier times and places. At that stage the issue is one of trance depth. However, when you reach a past life, another problem of recall may become evident to you. This has to do with those few clients who produce faulty memories due to outright conscious interference. This matter of tainted reports needs to be cleared up before you proceed into spiritual regression.

After regressing your subject into a past life, you must be watchful in checking to see if the client is recalling this life solely from historical details stored during their current lifetime. They may be using their imagination because of a conscious attraction to certain well-known events and familiar myths. Here bias enters the picture. I call this phenomenon the Atlantis Attraction because so many people are attracted to this story. You could first encounter this situation at intake when the client states, "I know we are going to find that I once lived in Atlantis." Their conviction centers around a desire to have once been part of a legendary early civilization on Earth.

There is nothing wrong with a client having conscious prior knowledge about world history because this may help in identifying scenes of the past. However, you should be aware that some aspects of the past, even those that are mythological, could be so attractive to the client that it drives memory and distorts recall. The use of client ideomotor signals to disrupt speech and thus disengage conscious thought interference is productive. I will illustrate an Atlantis Attraction case as an example:

Facilitator: Where are you now?

Subject: I'm in Atlantis.

Facilitator: All right—let's stop for a moment. I want you to take your time here and think carefully about what you have just told me. We won't speak to each other again until you have reviewed all your memories to verify that you are in Atlantis. After you have finished your examination of just where you are, I want you to notify me by raising the fingers of your right hand. I will not speak again until I see your fingers move.

Subject: (after a long pause and raising fingers) Oh . . . I guess I was wrong about Atlantis, but I seem to be a native on a beautiful island in the middle of an ocean.

I will have more to say about Atlantis under the section Reviewing Past Life Incarnations, particularly with regard to hybrid souls.

Another term I use for faulty reporting is the Famous Person Syndrome. Clients in this category want to be famous people. Most past life practitioners have had a number of clients who stated they were famous people before further examination revealed this was not true. In one of my three Marilyn Monroe cases, my client subsequently found she was a housekeeper for the actress. This client's preconceptions were unraveled when I asked her to go back to a scene where other people were around Marilyn Monroe and I told her to identify each person, with my client as part of the scene.

In life between lives regression, the good news is that once in the spirit world the conscious mind does not seem to interfere to any great degree with the superconscious except when reviewing past life incarnations. A primary example of conscious interference that I deal with in LBL work with a small percentage of clients is reports near the first stop into the spirit world where the client spontaneously states they are blue lights and therefore highly advanced. I did not have this problem before my books were published.

Truths may initially be clouded by desired fantasies, strong belief systems, repressed fears, or simply unhappiness with a current life the client thinks is dull. Memories that you suspect are faulty through conscious misconceptions can be handled by gentle challenging or critical questioning. In past life and life between lives regression you should avoid lengthy, complex questions directed at the subject. While you want to encourage them to elaborate about what they see and feel, as the facilitator your questions ought to be short, simple, and direct.

The secret to gaining accurate information is persistence and crosschecking. Moving back and forth in various time frames while going over the same ground is effective. Checking and reviewing their reports for consistency is very helpful to the subject as well. If you guide your subject carefully into their altered states and work through their perceptions and interpretations during past life recall, by the time the client reaches the gateway to the spirit world they will be much better prepared for accurate reporting.

My comments about faulty reporting may lead some people to question the validity of the whole process of hypnotherapy. This would be a wrong assumption because in my experience only a small portion of my clients have any real conscious interference. People do not deliberately lie under hypnosis. Some, however, may misrepresent what they believe to be the truth.

In most instances conscious thought works in our favor. Take the issue of recalling geographic locations and dates. Critics of past life regression ask how someone reliving a life during ancient times can give us an accurate fix of where they are on a current map of the world. The answer lies in the fact that the conscious mind retains a modern knowledge of both geography and time frames. I am not saying recalling this information is made easy by the conscious mind. With dates I often ask the client to visualize the numbers and then read them off to me one at a time.

The following case demonstrates a confusion with dates that centered around mental interference involving shame and guilt from a past life. I had a client who was a thirty-two-year-old Jewish woman born in 1964. In her immediate past life she had been an Austrian soldier persecuting Jews in a concentration camp during World War II. In that life she was born in 1920. When I asked, "How old were you when you died?" she said (much too quickly), "Eighty six." I realized this answer would have made her still alive in 2006, years beyond the time of our session. After challenging her, we learned that following the war this former Nazi soldier committed suicide at age forty-two (in 1962) from remorse over his savage acts against Jews. Two years later this soul reincarnated as the person who would eventually be my Jewish client.

On the other side of the coin, there are positive signs indicating credibility in recall to look for while you conduct your investigations. The following are three examples:

A. Is the subject having an uncommon and disturbing experience over gender? A male subject could be reliving a former life as a female or vice versa. The internal struggle with your client here lends validity to the entire experience.
B. Is there uncertainty in the beginning of a past life recall about the unfolding scene, which then evolves into a firm conviction? This is an indication of careful deliberation by the subject as they process their uncertainty (as with the case of Andy and Otis, cited earlier).
C. Is there an emotional change from flat reporting to more intense feelings of personal involvement? This transfer means

your subject is moving from detachment into more of a state of actual participation.

In the section under client preconceptions, I discussed outside influences prior to the LBL session from the perspective of both client and therapist. However, during the session itself conscious interference should be frequently monitored by checking on trance depth. For example, at the gateway a depressed client, filled with religious insecurities and feelings of unworthiness might expect to be taken to some dark, hellish place if their human psyche was still dominant. Asking your subject for clarifications based upon their own true inner wisdom, or perhaps working through a deeply bonded soulmate or spirit guide at the gate begins the process of reducing psychological disruptions by ego-filtering. This allows the subject to further dissociate from their temporary personality in this life in favor of their permanent soul identity. Generally, by the time your subject is in a deep superconscious state and recalling experiences from the spirit world, the higher soul-self is now in dominance and conscious interference will be greatly diminished or extinguished.

Part Four
THE MENTAL GATEWAY INTO THE SPIRIT WORLD

18

Past Life Death Scenes

At the moment of death in a former life, I place my hand on the forehead of my client and declare:

> You have just died and because you have been through this experience many times before, I want you to move away from your body, feeling free, with no more physical pain or discomfort.

The contact from my hand is intended to be a soothing energy transfer to engender acceptance and confidence.

I appeal to the calm observer, more detached aspect of their mind by reminding the subject that this death is over and the life completed. At the same time, it is not my intention to soften too much of the actual drama of being in a body at one moment and out the next because I want the client to experience vivid feelings in the first scene where they see themselves floating in a free soul-state. Not only is every client different in the way they express their visualizations, feelings, and emotions in death scenes, but these same people have altered sensations between death scenes from life to life.

Before proceeding beyond the death scene, I think it is appropriate to discuss the possible need for desensitization or deprogramming for the emotionally participating subject who is actually feeling the pain of a violent death to such an extent they may be inhibited from going further.

19

Desensitizing Trauma

Since desensitization is taught in most hypnotherapy courses for current and past life trauma, I will focus more on its applications to life between lives therapy. Emotional trauma from a death scene, such as suddenly being killed, can hinder a subject from moving away from their body. Surprisingly, most of your clients won't be inhibited in this way. Especially with your help, the average client realizes they are in a soul state and cannot be hurt anymore. They want to move on. It is because most subjects do desire a quick release from a death scene that you will be able to rapidly move them away from their body. But what if this does not happen?

The purpose of desensitization is to take a traumatic event or repressed incident and allow the mind to digest it slowly in order to live without panic, fear, anxiety, or discomfort. In traditional hypnotherapy, the current life event causing psychological problems is approached in stages, starting with mild versions. The client is then progressively advanced to more potent versions and finally to the source of the anxiety itself. The concept involves reliving the event to inhibit the emotional fight-or-flight reflex and thus bring about emotional reframing so the client acquires a sense of personal safety in the present.

Certainly, as an LBL therapist you will encounter situations where deprogramming a negative body imprint from a former life will be part of the service you can render a client. For instance, I had a client who was unable to wear a watch or bracelets on her wrists because in her last life she had been tied with leather thongs by the hands to a post in the desert and left to die. Before she died in agony, she had struggled so hard to free herself that the bones of her wrists were exposed after the flesh was torn away. I desensitized this terrible scene. This was not required to get her to leave her body for the spirit world but rather to alleviate the source of a physical discomfort today.

I am not one of those therapists who believe it is necessary for the subject to be returned to a gruesome scene and made to suffer by living through it all over again. My approach is to allow the client to visualize the overall negative aspects of the event as a detached observer, while still recognizing their feelings. I have found this to be sufficient because the details of the incident have been brought to a level where they can be analyzed rationally to expunge the trauma. I believe this method is especially appropriate for LBL therapy. I often rapidly move through a past life death scene and have the client hover over their body in the soul state. The client is then able to integrate the painful elements connected with the traumatic scene more effectively because in the soul state they have an awareness of their immortal self. Also, from the spirit world it is easier and more effective to look at other lives. If necessary we can return to a significant earlier life to locate the origins of a continually scarring karmic pattern.

I will take up the therapeutic aspects of soul healing later under Therapeutic Opportunities During Council Visitations in Part Five. Suffice it to say that recalling physical and emotional events about former lives when the subject is mentally out of body allows them to reach core issues related to karma, dissect them and expose them to examination for meaning and purpose. Spiritual regression is a powerful mechanism for the release of latent trauma because so much about our existence involves personal choices we make as souls and the reasons behind them.

20

Initial Visualizations of the Soul State

During a difficult death scene, or at the moment when a subject explains they have just died in a past life, I often mentally place an energy field of golden, protective light around them. At the same time, I announce to the client that their personal spirit guide is well aware they have died and is nearby. Then I say to my subject:

> You have just physically died and as you move out of your body you will be able to continue to talk to me and answer my questions because you are now in touch with your inner, true self. Feel your mind expanding into the highest levels of your being. Looking down at your body you may perceive some brief sadness at this moment but your spirit has been through this experience before and now you are able to return home. You can just float away when you are ready, leaving all physical pain and discomfort behind.

At this point I change the tempo of my questions and drop the level of my voice tone. Now I move more slowly, especially with a younger soul, and my questions are very deliberate. After all, your subject has just come face to face with their immortal ego and they need some time to adjust to being in a disembodied state. Keep in mind that in past life regression it is easier for the subject to be moved from body to body, from life to life, as opposed to having no body at all in their life between lives. This is because your subject, after all, is still a physical being.

If a client tells you, "I am moving out of my body but I don't know where I am!" simply reassure them that everything is normal. I would then add, "While I remain silent, just look around and report back the first thing you see."

You will find that most souls are usually on the ceiling of the room where they died or hovering over their body if death occurred outside.

The following series of open-ended questions are examples of what I ask the client at a death scene:

1. Where are you now in relation to your body?
2. Is anyone in the room (or near your body if outside)?
3. (If the answer is yes) Tell me about this person (or persons) near you. Who are they?
4. What do you see around you? (or What are you aware of?)
5. What are you feeling?
6. What is happening now? Then what happens? What is happening that you haven't yet told me about?
7. How do you feel about your death?

As I have said, if the client did not expect to die at that particular moment they may resist moving away from their body because of sadness or unfinished business. Perhaps they died while still quite young, or were surprised by a sudden accident, or were murdered. Still, desensitization is often unnecessary. In these cases I remind the subject that they probably knew in advance this life would be short and when they arrive home they will be able to talk to their guides about the circumstances. Unless they are inexperienced souls, the average client adjusts rather quickly to any sort of physical death.

With most clients, I find it is best to keep them suspended near their body while giving them time to collect their thoughts. This is the time for reassuring your subject if they seem confused or disoriented. Once a soul is oriented to the entire death scene I rapidly summarize what we have learned about their immediate past life. The client may wish to correct something they said to me about the life and the people in it. Now we have the opportunity to talk about the ultimate purpose of this life. Certainly, you could wait until later to review the life just lived, but I find this is a potent time to discuss whether they feel the life was a success or not in terms of preplanned goals. Since they have just finished mentally being in a past life, the scenes are still vivid and may have ramifications in their life today.

There will be more time during the client's orientation and debriefing to cover the life just lived in greater detail should you wish to do so. I plan to review the client's overall progress in all their former lives thoroughly at other places in the spirit world, particularly during their appearance in front of the council. I do not wish to delay the session for very long at the death scene and yet this time of reflection allows the subject space to adjust and visualize themselves as a soul while they are still near their body. I feel this is an added benefit for an immediate past life review.

Once a client visualizes their soul leaving the body, but while they are still in Earth's astral plane, an extremely rare phenomenon in spiritual regression may occur that is known as spirit attachment. I am often asked about "soul attachment and releasement" by LBL practitioners because so much has been made of this topic in metaphysical writing, some of which is unnecessarily sensationalized.

On very rare occasions, your LBL client's first visualizations of the spirit realm will involve seeing a disturbed spirit close by them. Your client may call them a "dark soul." Typically, this unhappy spirit is related to your client by blood, or they could be a spouse or friend. They may have nothing to do with a client's past life since we have now passed into the now time of the spirit world. Most clients who have this uncommon experience are just rather curious about what is going on. However, other highly susceptible people—many of whom have preconceptions (often from religious indoctrination as children) about the existence of "demonic, malevolent forces" around us—could react negatively to the experience.

In those infrequent situations where it becomes necessary to take action in dealing with a "lost soul" that is interfering with your client's movement into the spirit world, you should begin with calming techniques. I would first explain that this spirit is not going to "possess" your subject, nor are they a demonic, evil force. This soul is unhappy and needs help because they are not yet ready to leave Earth. You will find they are generally obsessed by an event at their death which they have not released, such as being murdered, committing suicide, or feeling troubled by a loved one they perceive is in danger. My views on this issue are expressed in Destiny of Souls under the section on demons or divas.

I would give your client gentle, appropriate suggestions such as the following:

> Let's relate to this troubled spirit by connecting with their energy field so we can find out who they are, what they want, why you are seeing them at this moment, and what you can do to help them move into the light.

One of my LBL colleagues wisely said, "While these entities may look, feel, and act like empirical entities, in most cases they represent personifications or archetypes from the client's own ongoing personal history as a soul."

21

Instructions for Soul Departure

In preparing the client for their withdrawal away from Earth, each therapist will want to design instructions to suit their own tastes and methodology. Perhaps you will need to employ variations in your standard procedure that would be more helpful to specific clients. Below are my own instructions, and their timing at this stage of the session is a serious consideration. Typically, I incorporate these instructions at the gateway. Nevertheless, with certain clients you might find soul-state instructions to be more effective if they are incorporated a little further along in the crossing phase. It depends on how much the subject is caught up in the moment. The instructions are in four parts:

1. You are now fully in a soul state, directly connected to the highest consciousness of your mind, which is like a vast computer holding all the stored knowledge of your entire existence. As an eternal, timeless being you have the ability to look forward and backward in physical time and be apart of any life you have ever lived before and to understand the events that shaped your immortal character. You will know the significant people who were with you in those lives and you will have the capacity to see these individuals as souls in the spirit world.

2. Soon you will remember details about your immortal life between lives and thus you will be able to respond to my questions about your life as a soul. You will have the

capability of discovering any aspect of your spiritual existence with objectivity and understanding. You also have the power to distinguish the difference between your immortal soul character and the personality and temperament of any physical body serving as your soul host in former lives and your current life.

3. We are now going to a place of expanded awareness as you move upward into the loving realm of an all-knowing spiritual power. Even though you are only now at the gateway to this beautiful realm, your soul can feel the joy of being released. Everything will become very familiar to you as we progress further because this peaceful realm embodies an all-knowing acceptance.

4. You are now going to move away from your body in perfect comfort. Soon, you will receive divine help in releasing all negative energy from your physical life. Remember, as you enter your eternal home think of it as a spiritual sanctuary of planning and harmony. It is also a place composed of wise and kind beings who have great love for you and want to help you in every way.

At the moment of crossing, the subject moves from linear to "now" time. Because of this change in perspective the entry is critical. It may be clear or hazy at first. There can also be entry variations with the same client in two different LBL sessions. An entry point in one LBL might involve arriving in a soul group while in another the client could find themselves in a spiritual library.

22

Phrasing Questions at the Gateway

Your subject has now had time to process to some extent their past life, the conditions surrounding their death, and they have listened to your instructions for departure. While the client may quickly realize they are physically dead, the adjustment to being a soul and having you move them through the spirit-world gateway goes more slowly. Part of this uncertainty lies in the fact that while your subject is mentally a spirit, they are reporting back to you from their current physical body.

For the average client, reporting from their soul-mind for the first time takes awhile to sort out. Earlier I mentioned that the sentient subject (representing perhaps some 15 percent of your clients) has difficulty with visualizations because they perceive through the senses. Up to now you will have had better results with the kinesthetic and auditory type of person by phrasing your questions in this way: "What are you sensing, feeling, hearing, or experiencing?" However, once they are fully in a soul state, reporting from out of their body, you will usually find many of these same people having an easier time responding to questions that center around the more typical "What are you seeing?"

Spiritual regression requires that you use your creative skills to suit the moment. Despite your directives to the client, they may not be ready to move at some juncture or have already moved on ahead of you. After physical death and a rapid review of their past life, I deliver the following series of questions involving choices:

1. As we prepare to move away from your body on your journey back home, do you wish to leave now or stay awhile to say goodbye to someone, or attend to other unfinished business on Earth?

This first question is significant because your subject may not be ready to leave Earth. The choice between going or staying immediately engages the subject to get into focus with an action they must take. While some souls may wish to say a mental goodbye to a loved one left behind, most elect to leave right away and will say, "I just want to go." An older, experienced soul might remark, "Oh, I'm free again! Great—I'm on my way home."

Even at this early stage of disembodiment, souls are aware they have the capacity to contact loved ones at any time. If your client elects to stay to bid goodbye to someone, you will want to travel with them and find out how they mentally touch this person. There are many techniques available to souls and I have detailed some of them in chapter two of Destiny of Souls. Essentially, the reason for this contact is to try and reassure the loved one that the departed soul-ego is still alive. Souls do not have the same overpowering grief about physical death as those who are left behind but many feel a duty to comfort.

Once the subject tells me they are ready to leave, I ask my follow-up questions:

2. As you move away from your body (through the roof inside a building, or directly into the sky if outside), please describe everything that happens so I can stay with you. (pause) Have you started to move?

There are clients who may not answer or they will give me a response that is vague and sketchy. Again, to encourage responses, your questions should pose choices.

3. Tell me, as you move away from Earth, can you see long stretches of countryside and towns (or the sea) below you, or is everything a blur?
4. Can you see the earth curved below you clearly, or is everything around you hazy?
5. As you leave do you feel any sort of pulling sensation, or not? Is it gentle or strong?
6. Are you moving upward and looking up, or does it feel like you are moving backward up a slide while looking down? (If the second condition, they will eventually turn around and experience the normal moving and looking up.)

I have found that while people are mentally traveling away from Earth's astral plane, it is necessary to keep them engaged and moving or the flow of information often tends to get bogged down. Critics of any sort of directive guidance caution against leading the client. These are valid concerns but I find that within this period of the session some subjects have a tendency to mentally dawdle. There are many reasons why they don't want to talk to you. Sometimes it is lack of confidence about reporting from the soul state. Perhaps they are mystified and a bit disoriented as souls with this experience. Quite possibly they are unable to respond well to you because what they are seeing represents divine immortality and it is so awesome they have difficulty communicating in a coherent fashion. There are also people who don't wish to interrupt their spiritual and emotional sensations with conversation. The best way I can describe these feelings of wonder is that the client is awakening to a new level of knowing.

Many clients at this stage seem passive when in fact most are intensely caught up in the action of crossing over. However, you need to know what is going on. Moreover, the client will be disappointed if this experience is not recorded on their audio cassette tapes. Another advantage of keeping these scenes at the gateway progressing vocally is the confidence people acquire by listening to you. They gain the sense that you know what is happening to them and that everything is quite normal. It is imperative that you convey the idea early on that you know your way around the spirit world and are familiar with all they are going through.

In establishing a spiritual rapport with your subject, you want them to explain as much as possible while at the same time avoiding any potential roadblocks over privacy. Occasionally, in the early stages a client will feel they might be violating some divine code of secrecy by revealing information. This is another reason why it is reassuring to the soul traveler to believe that you have been this way with many others before. While your questions should be delivered with self-assurance, they should also be asked respectfully and with deference to the sanctity of the spirit world.

To be honest, there is the tendency with some subjects not to work hard with spiritual recall at the crossing-over stage in their session because they expect it will come easily, and if it doesn't then you can make spiritual scenes materialize for them. If a client states, "I am not seeing anything right now," you must determine if they are fogging because of a lack of effort or because of actually having trouble with visualization. This kind of response must be evaluated by the use of persistent but gentle and accommodating questioning.

I have stated that during spiritual recall the margins between being a participant rather than an observer are often indistinct, as opposed to past life recall. In the soul state there is a melding of eternal timelines and your questions should liberate the subject to project their own associations plainly. There are three types of questions that are useful here:

A. The open-ended question: "Give me your first impression of where you are in relation to your surroundings."
B. The elaboration question: "How do you feel about all this? Are you happy or sad? Are you excited, or unsure of how

you feel? What does this mean to you? What is it you are trying to tell me? Help me to understand what you are seeing and feeling."
C. Repeating and summarizing questions: "Now that you have told me so-and-so, let me review what you have said. Have I got it right? Is there anything you wish to add?"

One of the most helpful comments you can offer a hypnosis subject who is struggling with visualizations is to broadly address the unconscious mind by stating something like: "Look to your own inner awareness and just take what is most needed at this state of your spiritual journey." Another way of phrasing this sort of question might be: "I want you now to go to that mental state that you find necessary in order to move to the place where you need to be." Sometimes generalized, even vague commands of this sort allow the client to decipher them to suit themselves and can be most effective. Finally, I cannot stress enough that you must give the subject time to answer questions completely while also keeping them moving with encouragement. This is a delicate balancing act and one that improves with experience. I tell my students not to become jaded when they do gain experience. Always show enthusiasm and treat each person as though you are captivated by their story. They need to feel that you are caught up with their visualizations by hearing such statements from you as, "Oh, really, it sounds wonderful. Please tell me more." Personally, I am fascinated by reports from the spirit world, regardless of how many times I hear the same descriptions. The experience of every client interests me, and so it should be with all professionals engaging in spiritual regression.

23

The Unresponsive LBL Client

There are subjects who can be taken all the way through a past life and then shut down at the gateway to the spirit world. If blocking is going to occur, it is more likely that it will happen when the client is trying to recover childhood memories, or during your attempt to move them into a past life, rather than at the gateway. Subjects who are blocking further hypnosis advancement at any of these junctures in their session may have to eventually be brought to a full awake state. They should always be handled with care. Hypnosis facilitators must be especially kind and understanding with aborted sessions.

Before these people leave my office I spend time discussing all the ramifications of their inability to proceed further and reassure them they are not failures because there are reasons behind everything in life. It is possible that at some future date they will be more successful.

There is a well-established technique in past life regression that is utilized when a subject is unable to visualize an opening scene of themselves in another time in a different body. The facilitator takes pressure off this struggle by simply saying:

> Don't try to analyze anything, just make up a story for me. I want you to begin by telling me the first thing that comes into your mind. Just pick a place and time and make things up as you go along.

Invariably, if a subject is able to follow these instructions, the actual past life begins to unfold slowly but quite naturally. It seems to bring about a release in their mind, as they are then more comfortable with my giving them permission to create any fantasy they wish. Unfortunately, I have not found this technique to be at all effective for spiritual recall with subjects in a superconscious state. This is probably due to the domination of a higher inner life soul self over any past life body at this stage in the LBL session.

With past life recall we work with the subconscious mind. In a soul state, the superconscious mind is even further distanced from conscious levels. A key aspect to client resistance and blocking related to spiritual regression is that in order to reach the immortal soul of your client in the superconscious, you must work through both the conscious and the subconscious mind. In combating blocking, life would be much easier for the spiritual regressionist if the various levels of the mind could be isolated and closed off when they get in the way. Of course, this we cannot do.

What does being in a soul state have to do with client resistance? The emotional temperament and intellectual brain of your client's current body may actually be inhibiting their immortal soul-character from expression between death and the crossing. Unconscious resistance may come from the difficulty of your subject in separating their temporary human personality from the permanent soul character, or ego, they also possess. There is a duality here and some clients find working through these two forces more difficult than others.

If you see that your subject's current personality is trying to answer for their soul identity and having difficulty with self-expression in the period right after death, there are ways in assisting them to bridge this gap. Naturally, additional deepening of the trance state is your first consideration. I would also suggest including such statements to the subject as the following:

You have moved to a place beyond your current personality where your character is more permanent. Yet, you are still who you are. Take three deep breaths and on the third breath you will go to a level where you need to be to recall who you really are as a soul, with all information related to your immortal identity.

I will have more to say about this topic in my section on Connections Between Body and Soul. As far as bridging the gap between the two egos of the soul and brain at this stage in the session there is another useful method to consider. Right after death from a former life, I allow the client to compare the temperament and personality of their current life with this former life. Both involve being in physical bodies. The sudden awareness of these differences may jump-start your subject into getting past any identity barriers leading to confusion over their current body and the soul.

Understandably, those clients who reach the spiritual gateway and cannot go further are the most disappointed. Some display anger while others have an attitude of resignation. There are those clients who become very emotional and cry. Quite often, if blocking has ended the session prematurely, the client will state, "I felt all along I was going to have obstructions and be prevented from receiving information about myself."

As I mentioned in the section on Client Preconceptions, there are people who set themselves up for disappointment. They may have unresolved fears about the session, such as uncovering unpleasant details about themselves that they don't really want to know. They lack trust in themselves and perhaps in you. Certainly, no hypnotherapist can guarantee a successful LBL session. We can only state that we will work diligently, in conjunction with the active participation by the client, to elicit spiritual information sought by them. I tell my LBL students they will have cases that must be aborted due to client blocking. Also, I should state you will have certain clients that you simply do not personally connect with at all. There are a number of reasons for this lack of rapport, not the least of which could be a polarity of negative energy between you.

Let me address your reaction to a client who is stuck at a particular place for deep psychological reasons. Try not to get caught up in your own LBL agenda as a facilitator if the client is struggling against the visualizations you suggest. Simply place everything on hold. If the client is blocking, or resisting all movement forward into the spirit world—or a past life, for that matter—rather than feeling personally thwarted and frustrated, see this situation as an opportunity for both of you to learn what is behind the problem therapeutically, no matter how long it takes. Subjects are like pilgrims, following the travels of their own psyche. Keep in mind that a block may have nothing to do with their depth of trance, your skill, or even the LBL session itself, but rather a manifestation of current feelings of distress in their body at this time and place in your office. In this situation, I would suggest such questions as: "Can you describe your feelings right now?" "What is your body trying to tell us that we both should know at this moment?" "Have you had what you are now experiencing before?"

I have found in some situations of this sort that the subject is unable to continue the LBL session as planned. Yet, what has transpired between client and therapist during the block can be very productive, creating beneficial psychological venting that fosters healing. When fully awake, follow-up processing is critical for the client's well-being. People will be disappointed that an LBL was not achieved. This is natural. However, when ramifications of why this happened are discussed and analyzed, the case may produce self-awareness, insight and understanding that is so valuable to the saddened client that they consider the aborted session a partial or full success. This person learned what they needed to know and later could well return for a fruitful LBL session.

24

Overcoming Specific Types of Client Blocking

Naturally, you will try to do everything possible to prevent aborting the session due to blocking, particularly if the cause is self-sabotage. My LBL students are hypnosis professionals with a variety of backgrounds and experience. Most feel, as I do, that many approaches may be utilized to clear the subject's energy field, such as shamanic or reiki techniques. I have often used hand passes combined with certain vibrations of my voice to interact with a subject's blocked energy. I mentioned placing my hand on the client's forehead to effect a positive energy transfer while giving release commands.

The following are illustrations of resistive statements that you might hear from subjects at the gateway. With each of these statements, I have listed an example of a metaphoric or symbolic response by the facilitator, which describes one image that is known applied to another as yet unknown. These images represent spiritual space that is obscured by the subject during the crossing. Symbolic comparisons often serve as comfortable release mechanisms from blocking.

1. **Subject:** I don't trust what I am seeing.
   Facilitator: Allow your imagination to take over and don't try to figure anything out at this moment. Your imagination is the key to the soul. This is your soul's way of talking with you.
2. **Subject:** I can't see anything but blackness.

Facilitator: You are an energy form. There is a light from your energy extending from your hands. Turn up the power with your mind and hold your hands out in front of you. This will show us the way and I will follow you (or take my hand and lead me), because you have been this way before.

3. **Subject:** I don't know what I am supposed to do.

   Facilitator: I want you to talk silently to your personal guide, who is nearby. Ask for advice from this wise being and then tell me what you have been told and where you will be taken next.

4. **Subject:** I seem to be drifting in a void that is bright in some places and dark in others, and I am stuck in limbo.

   Facilitator: I want you to consider this void in total for me as if you were drifting over a huge black-and-white-checkered chessboard with chess pieces. You are one of those pieces who can move in any direction. An unseen hand is now directing you to a certain place. See yourself going there. (pause) Now describe to me where you are being taken.

5. **Subject:** I am not sure if I am supposed to say anything to you.

   Facilitator: You can say or do anything you want because these memories belong to you, since they are in your soul-mind. You can give yourself permission to respond to my questions in any way you see fit. I am with you because you want my help. Think of yourself as a movie projectionist with the ability to show me your pictures and move them fast or slow, with the action taking place in your mind.

Notice in my response to this last question concerning privacy I did not suggest to the subject that we actually stop this line of inquiry, only that we could proceed either slowly or quickly. If the concern over soul privacy lessens, I will try and work around it gently with coaxing. The whole idea is to avoid direct confrontation by giving the subject permission to self-actualize through releasing what is being held by their soul memory.

25

Blocking by the Client's Guide

This is a very delicate area for the spiritual regressionist. When a client forcefully states, "I am being blocked from going further," I suspect a guide is at work. If you believe information is being blocked in some way by a spirit guide, it generally means this person has not progressed to the stage in life where they are supposed to have certain information. This individual's guide may not want to preempt self-discovery. Perhaps a major fork in life has not yet been reached and a guide feels choices need to be made without advance coaching. This is one reason why I eventually stopped seeing most clients under age thirty. Moreover, there are personal guides who want the amnesiac block we are given at birth regarding who we really are, and our purpose, to remain in place for a lifetime because it serves our best interests.

However, because I am stubborn I do not give up easily when I presume blocking is coming from a guide. I try to discover the specific area that my client's guide wishes to avoid and work around it rather than assuming this teacher does not want their student to see anything whatsoever. I may place myself in a light trance state and with closed eyes call upon my own spiritual guide to assist me in reasoning with my subject's guide to partially remove blocks in appropriate areas.

I do this if I believe my client, for their mental well-being, is desperate for the information. I may or may not feel my own guide is assisting me with the case. Thus, I always appeal directly to the blocking guide and tell my client to do the same. One permission technique I find to be effective is to request that my client repeat each line of the following petition out loud after me:

> I ask that you release the barriers to my mind so I can assume greater responsibility for my life with this knowledge. I am ready to face the real truth about myself. I ask that you trust Michael (use your name here) as someone who wishes to help me realize my potential and will respect and protect what information you choose to give me about my life in the spirit world.

Thankfully, total blocks from guides are not all that common. It is best to learn early on the true origins of any blocks. Do they come from the subject, or from a guide through the subject? While blocking can occur at any time in a session, once your client mentally crosses into the spirit world, usually your major worries are over. I find that blocking guides manifest themselves strongly right after a past life death and before the crossing into the spirit world is completed. Thus, if there is to be an impediment, quite often it will take place at the gate. When I train LBL students, they like to hear examples of predicaments and solutions. To illustrate a situation with a blocking guide for this text, I have chosen the following edited case I call the Apache Scout. This involves my subject, Kyle, and his guide, Adia.

One of the most confusing aspects of life's paths is the difficulty in making choices in our love relationships. These choices are usually far more complex than career or financial decisions. I rank the pain from a lost love as a consequence of certain decisions at the top of emotional trauma. Quite often, right after a death sequence a client's full engagement with his or her soul will produce haunting responses about people they have known and loved. Hypnosis sessions are likely to come to an abrupt halt while the subject processes this information, which may elicit negative self-images and a vital personal mission that has been disrupted. This was the situation with Kyle.

Kyle was a thirty-seven-year-old white-water rafting instructor whose personal history included a desire for outside employment coupled with freedom and adventure. During intake he sat nervously in my office, wishing our session could be one of physical endurance rather than "washing out the negativity in my mind," as he put it. Kyle's fists were clenched as he told me about an impending divorce from Diane, his high-school sweetheart. She told Kyle she was sick of his being gone all the time on long rafting trips with clients. Diane wanted him to "grow up, settle down, get a local job, and stop being an absentee father and husband." Kyle's increased drinking habits added to his marital discord.

The separation had been very difficult for both parties, with intense anger and blame over money, lifestyle, and the children. Recently, Kyle had started dating Linda, a woman he had met at Alcoholics Anonymous. While their relationship was developing, Kyle was growing more confused and frustrated with the changes in his life because he still loved Diane. His wife told Kyle she would never stop loving him but refused to reconcile their marriage because he would not stay home.

Although Kyle's hypnosis session proceeded on course, it did not go easily due to his restlessness and preoccupation. Once into Kyle's past life we learned he had been a scout for a U.S. Army cavalry unit in the Arizona desert. His name was Hal and he was killed at age thirty-nine in 1873 by Apache Indians during a raid on his party. At the moment Kyle visualized his death as Hal, he began shaking uncontrollably. My attempts to calm him down were fruitless.

Dr. N: Tell me what is bothering you the most right now. Is it the pain of your death and the fact you are only thirty-nine—or something else?

Kyle: (tearfully, taking rapid, short breaths) No, no, it's Jane . . . DAMN, SHE WAS RIGHT! She knew I was going to be killed by the Apaches.

Dr. N: Who is Jane?

Kyle: My wife . . . she didn't want me to go on this trip . . . and now look . . . I HAVE ABANDONED HER—and my three children.

Dr. N: But isn't scouting Indians your job? The way you earn your living? Was there something different about this particular assignment?

Kyle: No, they are all dangerous—but I had recently become a small rancher, just to please Jane. I promised her that I would settle down and do no more work for the army. Yet I missed the life so much—not being tied down—the adventure—new things happening every day—the camaraderie of the men . . .

Dr. N: So, why did you decide to work once again with the army on this particular trip?

Kyle: Major Henderson came to me, requesting my aid, and offered me extra money. Jane pleaded with me. She said she had a premonition about something bad that would happen. She reminded me of my promise to her . . . but I went anyway.

Dr. N: Could Major Henderson have found someone else?

Kyle: (long pause) Yes, I suppose so, but I was good and the Major was pressed for time. Oh, Jane . . . I'm sorry . . .

Dr. N: Who is Jane in your current life?

Kyle: (tearfully) She is Diane.

As I began my instructions for Hal to move away from his body in the Arizona desert toward the gateway, he cried out, "I'm stuck—I feel something is preventing me—restricting me ..."

When I found it impossible to move Hal from the scene of his death, I suspected that while he was reluctant to leave Jane, my client's subconscious mind was combining his conscious resistance over not wanting to abandon Diane. Both conscious and subconscious memories were preventing him from moving into a superconscious state due to powerful feelings of remorse and guilt. We were somewhere between the Arizona desert and the gate to the spirit world. I decided to request help from my client's guide. After a few moments of meditation, I continued:

Dr. N: I am going to call upon your guide to come to us in this time of trial. Imagine that when you look down you see the Arizona desert, but when you turn upward you can see a protective light waiting. I want you to picture yourself as floating while this room is superimposed over the whole scene so all of us can participate. I am now going to call upon this protective light force above you to come down and help us. This is your personal spirit guide who is loving and forgiving. Will you allow me to do this and assist me?

Kyle: (tentatively) Yes, but I don't know . . .

Dr. N: (after continued encouragement) Good. Now, on the count of three, your guide is going to float down to you and you will be able to describe this being to me very clearly. Ready! (I place my hand on Kyle's forehead) One, two, three! What do you see?

Kyle: (long pause) Oh . . . he is here . . . an older man . . . thin . . . long, grayish hair . . .

Dr. N: What does his face look like?

Kyle: Wise . . . he looks stern—no, challenging.

Dr. N: What is his name?

Kyle: A . . . Adia. He is here.

Dr. N: I feel his presence, too, and this is good, because we could use his assistance right now. I want you to concentrate hard. What does Adia say to you as a telepathic message for your mind?

Kyle: Please don't talk for a minute.

Dr. N: (after a moderate wait) Well . . . ?

Kyle: I . . . can't . . . (subject begins to shake)

Dr. N: (loudly, in a commanding tone, allowing no further time for the subject to disengage) Speak for Adia using your own voice, now!

Kyle: (in a strange, low, and very controlled voice) You were brought here at this time to work with this man (me) in order to understand what choices you have made (as Hal and Kyle). I will allow you to know certain things (at this point in time) but not others because your choices (with the soul of Jane and Diane) are still open to you.

I have condensed much of this phase of the case for brevity. We were able to learn that Diane is Kyle's primary soulmate. Little else of Kyle's spiritual life was revealed to him. Kyle's session was invaluable, however, because he now understood Diane's decision to leave him involved all the old issues of her former abandonment as Jane. The karmic lesson here is not one of punishment but rather to offer understanding about the consequences of our choices as they affect others in many lifetimes. Kyle's long-term goals in this life, his spiritual life, and his future with Diane were all being blocked because he is in the middle of a testing period—at a crossroads in his current life.

All blocking by guides has purpose. To enable Kyle to see other members of his spirit group, experience a meeting with his council, and review his choice of his current body in the life selection room would have circumvented crucial elements of decision-making at this time in Kyle's life. Notice that the ages (thirty-seven and thirty-nine) for major decisions concerning abandonment in both his last and current lives are about the same. Timelines represent multiple causality.

The ripples of timelines in our existence present echoes of opportunity. Each path has the potential for learning with regard to our major contracts in life. Kyle came away from our session knowing the problem, without being given answers to that problem. He acquired more acceptance of the notion that all life experiences have meaning. Kyle trusted that his blocking guide only wanted him to know what was best for him right now in his life.

There are several more points about spiritual guides and LBL work you might consider. A facilitator should be cautious of initial client reporting about messages from their guide at the gateway. Some clients might superimpose their own mentality or belief system for that of their guide. It is not common at this stage, but prior fears, misconceptions or expectations on the conscious level may intrude to such an extent that actual messages from the subject's spirit guide are not getting through. This will usually disappear as the session progresses deeper into the spirit world. Your task in these early stages after the crossing is to isolate your client's thought processes from that of their guide by challenging the client's interpretation of guide responses by your questions. You need to know if the client is screening or interpreting information to comfort themselves in some self-protective manner.

On the other hand, if your client is genuinely having trouble with connecting to an unseen guide for whatever reason, I would suggest an alternate approach such as simply bypassing the spirit guide and working with another being in the spirit world. This could be an Archivist Soul in the library, or an Elder on the soul's Council. Always keep in mind that spiritual teachers exist on many levels and they often engage in Socratic methods of self-discovery as opposed to giving direct answers to questions asked of them. At times you will feel your client is being directed by an outside force of some sort.

26

Visions of Light and Darkness While Crossing

Let's return to those clients who have done well with their departure from Earth's astral plane and have floated past the gateway. At this stage you will want to continually check on their surroundings. During the crossing, my next series of questions begins with the following:

1. As you find yourself moving higher and higher and further and further away from Earth, does the space around you get lighter or darker?

While this may seem like a simple question, it is one filled with ramifications, depending upon the experience of the soul involved. When a client tells me, "I pass immediately into bright light," I can usually predict this is a mature, fast-moving soul who is eager to get home. At the same time, I assume that the intelligent force pulling the soul knows exactly the rate of departure speed which will best accommodate this soul's ability to adjust to rapid changes following physical death. Souls who are less certain about where they are move more slowly. On the other hand, there are souls who wish to move gradually into the spirit world, regardless of their state of advancement.

I don't have any set formula I can offer as to why some souls see a portal or tunnel they must pass through while others go straight into the light. I do know the rate of transmigration is connected to the circumstances of death and familiarity with the spirit world. There are accounts from a few NDEs who have had a less than positive experience with temporary death because they saw only darkness. They report being stuck in a tunnel and returning back to life without even seeing a loving light coming toward them. This can happen when the death experience is especially brief at the gateway, followed by a return to life. Most NDEs remember feeling love and seeing only bright light.

What is important here is that when your client tells you they are drifting through darkness or floating within gray, misty veils, or a fleecy, cloudlike atmosphere where they can't see anything, just calmly keep them moving and reassure the subject that everything is normal. Regardless of the responses as to light or darkness, I tell my clients:

2. You have been this way before. Just keep moving and accept the fact that a loving power is taking you to a safe place.

I explain that soon they are going to experience scenes where they are part of the action, just as they did during their past life recall. The difference is that now they have an ethereal body of pure energy, but with the same ability to keep reporting their memories back to me through their current physical body. For more information, I urge you to review chapter two in Journey of Souls where I cite three cases of souls crossing into the spirit world. Their accounts range from amazement to matter-of-fact reporting. The diversity of such entries gives us perspective. At this juncture, I ask the subject:

3. Tell me when you can see far into the distance beyond your immediate surroundings.

This is one of those moments when your silence is especially helpful to the subject. I may then ask for an ideomotor response such as:

4. Take your time. Move the fingers of your right hand when you can see into the distance.

I want this signal to come spontaneously and directly from the superconscious mind without any critical conscious analysis. You must wait until the subject is ready to report or there could be a tendency to push the visualization just to satisfy the facilitator.

Once the subject tells me they have floated into a space where they can see into the distance, it does not matter if they see brightness all around them or a hazy, darkened glow. I ask everyone the same type of question about individual lights:

5. Do you see a large globe of light near you, or do you see points of light off into the distance?

Once again, the use of alternative choices alleviates client resistance and, with some, perhaps a little anxiety about being lost in space. Nevertheless, subjects will answer truthfully if they see something different from your suggestions. This is fine because you want to keep the subject talking and on track.

Sooner or later most subjects will report seeing lights. I may or may not explain that these lights represent intelligent beings. Only with a very uncertain client will I engage in coaching here. A larger, single globe of light near the soul typically represents a spirit guide, while points of light in the distance are frequently companions from their spirit group. Clients may experience slightly different spiritual visualizations after each life. For instance, a guide may be waiting near the gate after one life but be located deeper into the spirit world after another. Soulmates may be in evidence at the crossing after one life but not the next.

27

First Contact with Spirits

When clients initially see lights in the distance, they often exclaim, "I see stars!" This is because their visions seem to represent a night sky on Earth. I will then continue with my series of questions related to the lights:

6. How many lights do you see? Count them.
7. Are they bunched together or spread out?
8. Does one seem larger than the rest?

Subjects often answer, "I see one big light globe far away." This usually represents a guide. Regardless of the type of response about lights, my next question is always the same:

9. Do you need to move to the right, continue straight ahead, or move left to intersect with this light (or lights)?

Besides giving them choices, this approach achieves excellent results because now your subject's directional compass kicks in and they become aware they have the ability to manage their own progress in the spirit world. Invariably, the client will answer that the lights are in one particular direction, and I simply tell them:

10. Float (right, left, or straight ahead) toward the light while the light floats toward you.

Certainly, there may be the need to pause here to let your client get their bearings, but it is important to keep them from getting mired down by taking too long to connect with the points of light. My next question is:

11. As the light comes close to you, and you move close to it, I want to know if it is bright or dim, and what colors you see.

If they are responsive, I will inquire about the core and halo colors of the light, which correlate with the level of advancement and character of the soul. This topic is detailed in Destiny of Souls (chapter five). I will review colors a bit more when we get to the section on Recognition of Soul Colors. If the subject sees just one bright globe or column of light in front of them, essentially I want to learn if the light is bright white, yellow, blue, or a light purple hue to give me an indication of whether we have a senior or junior guide on the scene. Two or more lights of varying colors clustered together often represent soul companions.

In my LBL classes, with students conducting spiritual regression on one another, I notice there is some confusion over the color white as it pertains to guides and soul companions. My students ask, "Why does the color white appear with both guides and younger souls?" This took me a while to unravel in my early years of LBL work. Color represents energy vibration and white is the base line for the rest of the color spectrum.

Clients reporting on lights moving toward them from a distance usually say, "I see white lights coming out of semi-darkness." This is why—at the first sighting—they frequently refer to these lights as stars. As you move your client closer to the lights, the scene changes, and I ask:

12. Please describe the shape and appearance of the light that has come to meet you.

If a guide is approaching, hypnosis subjects often see a large ball of white light, an elongated shape, or a human figure. After a short time your client may then tell you that the white light has altered to a yellow or bluish color. However, this kind of reporting about alterations from a brilliant white to another color might not be given until later in the session, when you take your subject into orientation or perhaps their spirit group.

If your client reports a steady, brilliant white light, this indicates a purity of vibrational energy that denotes clarity of thought and intentions. These are the marks of an advanced soul along with the knowledge and wisdom that emanate from the blue and violet hues. While flecks of white can also emerge in the reds, yellows, greens, and blues, typically, you will find that the younger souls display only a constant white. These white tones may appear dim or fluctuating in luminosity. Flickering lights often represent an essence of restlessness, excited enthusiasm, and the striving for harmony so characteristic of less advanced souls.

When there is a convergence of the soul and the light that comes to meet them, I will ask:

13. Does this light drift close to you, as if taking you by the hand, or does it seem to envelop you with loving energy?

Please refer to Destiny of Souls, chapter four, in my section on soul treatment near the gateway. There is a difference in technique when a guide envelops the soul in healing energy or simply focuses on the edges of the soul's etheric body, such as taking the soul's hand. Envelopment (where the soul feels they are in a bubble) is almost always executed by a spirit guide rather than a primary soulmate or companion soul.

Next, I might inquire about how a guide's energy makes my client feel. It is here when rejuvenating energy is applied to the returning soul through a process I call permeation, where healing energy passes through the soul. I review the various forms of spiritual energy restoration under chapter four in Destiny of Souls. During this phase of the session you will find that most clients are going to begin to relax. Responses vary from a sense of complete awe to one of peace. Subjects have the feeling that suddenly their energy is less dense. This is an indication that they have mentally separated from their physical body.

When people see their guides for the first time in your office, be prepared for an emotional response. Many become tearful or break down and cry over being in the presence of this loving teacher who has been assigned to them. Other clients will laugh for joy at what they are seeing and feeling after recognizing their guide. Frankly, this is one of the most profound moments in your session so I would recommend you allow your clients to savor it without much talking from you. Have a box of facial tissues handy. It is my habit to give post-hypnotic suggestions so that the memories of these mental images of their personal guide will remain for the rest of their lives.

28

Interaction with Welcoming Spirits

The recognition and personal dynamics with spirits who have traveled near the gate to meet the incoming soul is most significant. I start this phase by asking an open-ended question:

1. Do you have any thoughts about this entity who has come to meet you that we have not discussed?

Most clients need a few moments to identify and respond to questions about their guides and soul companions. Somewhere in the context of this questioning you should ask:

2. Do you have a sense that the being in front of you appears as a male or a female?

I find that souls who continue to see only a mass of genderless light are often more experienced and really don't need the comfort of seeing a human figure. You will have clients who report that many spirits appear to be androgynous.

If the light is a soul companion, they will generally provide instant recognition by revealing a physical body from a former life or even someone in the client's life today. Anytime the client sees a human form, irrespective of whether the spirit is a guide or soulmate, I will ask the following types of questions:

3. Can you see any facial features?
4. How about hair color and length? Eye color?
5. Does this being have a full-body outline that looks like anyone you know?

6. I realize no earthly speech sounds exist in this place, but are you receiving any telepathic communications we should talk about, either with words or by visual pictures placed in your mind?

In Journey of Souls, listed under homecoming in chapter three, I cite cases that explain what it is like for a client to meet members of their spirit group near the gateway. Typically, such encounters involve only a primary soulmate. Should such a meeting occur, it never seems to last long because normally a guide is ready to take over and conduct the returning soul to their next station. If there is to be an elaborate celebration involving many soul companions, this will usually take place later when a returning soul makes first contact with their entire cluster group. Any sort of homecoming with members of a spirit group, either at the gateway or within the cluster, is designed to honor the soul with love and rejoicing.

Homecoming gatherings can have profound meanings aside from all the fun and games. As an example, I had a client whose immediate past life involved a close association with four friends in the same British Army unit who were sent to France at the beginning of World War I. In late August, 1914, these five comrades had a final dinner together at a colorful Paris café located on the left bank of the Seine. There was music, wine, singing, and revelry while they tried to forget what lay ahead. The next morning these soldiers were posted to the front lines and in early September, on the same day and hour, all but one died on the battlefield in the First Battle of the Marne. The sole survivor was badly wounded and invalided home. For the rest of his pain-filled life he mourned for the loss of his friends and felt guilt that he alone had survived. This soldier was my client and he died in that life in 1936.

Upon returning to his spirit group, his four friends met him, dressed in their uniforms, and held a homecoming reunion with a re-created scene from the Paris café. This particular homecoming was intended to bring release from the tragedy of the past life as a means of enhancing the healing process. While it is true that souls have energy restoration available to them near the gate, there appears to be something more offered to souls returning home after certain traumatic events. I find this is especially true where lovers and dear friends are lost. Thus, while homecoming scenes can be utilized just for pleasure, be aware that they may be symbolic of poignant karmic events that have a special meaning to your client. There is the possibility these past life events are impacting the client today.

Please keep in mind that it does not matter if a loved one from the past life you have just reviewed with your client is still living on Earth in the same time frame. This is because a part of our energy never leaves the spirit world. For example, if your mother died thirty years before you—even if she has reincarnated into a new life—part of her energy left in the spirit world is always available to welcome you back. This process in described in Destiny of Souls on many pages under soul division.

During the time spirits are identified at any portion of your spiritual regression session, it is always best to move slowly to give the subject time for recognition. When it comes to communication with guides, initially you should be prepared for sketchy responses. Because the relationship between your client and their teacher is so intense, they may simply divert your questions by responding, "We have nothing to say to each other." What this really means is they have nothing to say to you. The conversation is considered too private or the client believes no words are necessary to describe what is transpiring.

I do not accept any client reticence passively. My job is to learn as much as I can for the client in their current life. I might gently remind them that I know communications with their guide are privileged and I honor this sanction. However, I could also add:

> It is important that you report back to me what you are receiving so that I will know that everything is all right.

Under some conditions, I might use a more forceful approach:

> You came to me to access spiritual information important to your current life and well-being and I need your assistance and cooperation in helping me with this task so it may be recorded (on their audio tapes).

If my client is still resistant about providing information with a spirit guide, I will simply continue my main line of questioning. This might be a good time to ask:

7. What is the name of your spirit guide?

During intake, I explained to the client that I would be touching their forehead with my fingers from time to time as a cause-and- effect energy transfer to assist with recall. Before hypnosis begins, I precondition the client by explaining that this procedure is very useful with names. At this point in the session, while executing this maneuver, I will state they can both sound out and spell the name for me to assist them in recall.

Working on a guide's name near the gate is useful preparation for the time in our session when I will ask about spirit names in the client's soul cluster group. Sometimes clients can spell spirit names easier than they can pronounce them. If the subject draws a blank about their guide's name, I will remark, "Don't worry about this, when you think of their name later you can just tell me."

If the client is able to answer any questions about receiving thoughts from their guide, I continue my investigations with:

8. What are you being told?

I might want to be more specific and push harder by asking:

9. How does your guide feel about your performance in the last life?

Lines of questioning and responses differ at this point with every client. However, you should know that normally not much information is acquired at the gateway. Usual responses here are "My guide is telling me I did what I needed to do" or "He is saying, 'Welcome back, we will talk soon.'"

Nevertheless, you are setting the stage for the client's conscious mind to accept the fact that they will be called upon by you to answer such questions in more detail further into the spirit world.

I never tarry too long near the gateway because I want to prod my client into moving along with their guide to the next station, where more information will be forthcoming. Possibly the first stop will be a space of soul energy restoration, but initially I try not to suggest areas where they might go, unless the client is mired down. To a question at this juncture that is phrased:

10. What is happening now?

The client often responds with, "I am moving again." If it seems to me that nothing is unfolding in the client's mind, I could suggest:

11. Do you feel you are ready to be taken somewhere?

One of the most common questions I ask throughout the session is:

12. Where are you being taken next?

Only if all else fails will I be more specific, such as:

Do you think it's time to go to some sort of orientation with your guide?

There is one other aspect about soul movement described by clients that should be recognized. Some clients who are caught up in the action of transporting themselves from place to place in the spirit world need only to form the thought and suddenly they are there. This is the essence of what seems to be the true nature of soul travel. Thus you may find that these clients are prone to get ahead of your instructions involving movement.

29

Station Stops for the Incoming Soul

Basically, there are three primary station stops for the incoming soul:

A. The gateway, when initial contact is made with another spirit.
B. Orientation, where the soul is taken to a space for debriefing by a guide.
C. A final stop, where the soul is returned to their own cluster group.

You will encounter variations in this format with certain clients that relate not only to the state of advancement of the soul but also to the amount of challenge or trauma involved in the life just lived. A soul may go directly to their spirit group or a Council of Elders and bypass a preliminary orientation. The soul may also experience a period of solitude and reflection in a quiet space without much contact with spirits. The more advanced souls who are involved with independent study groups might rejoin them immediately upon returning from an incarnation. Then, too, there are those souls who return from a life and go at once into a classroom situation or a library for study. What returning souls do not do is immediately reincarnate into another life.

For the newly discarnate soul, by far the most common deviation from the standard three primary stops is an immediate assignment to a place of energy restoration. There are souls who require emergency treatment to restore their damaged energy as soon as possible. While most initial meetings and orientation with guides involve some sort of on-the-spot rejuvenation of energy, this healing process has many alternative procedures in the spirit world.

Sometimes a client who has just crossed over will tell you their weakened soul energy is in a strange-looking space. For instance, they could tell you they are in a geometric or crystalline enclosure that seems to be assisting them in healing and balancing their energy. They might comment about the need to fine-tune their vibrational levels with the help of these surroundings and that they need solitude before rejoining their spirit group. They don't wish to mentally communicate with anyone for a while. It would seem after some lives souls must have a sanctuary for quiet reflection before they can face any other activities. Clients do say, however, that guides monitor their progress.

Clients often discuss crystals as a symbol of rejuvenation. Be prepared to hear from your client that these spaces of energy healing appear to resemble glasslike prisms or multifaceted walls reflecting colored lights all around them. Such spaces may function as vibrational generators to recharge the natural energies of the soul through a universal healing energy. Occasionally I will place a quartz crystal into the hand of a client who is trying to articulate what is going on because I believe the crystal can serve as a conductor of thought patterns between us.

In life, as well as life between lives, the benefits of solitude provide a time for self-evaluation and inspiration through personal energy restoration. During life we can become so distracted by the roles we play that we never learn who we really are. After a particularly difficult life, we suddenly find ourselves lacking the body that bonded us to all the challenging circumstances we faced. One can imagine the necessity for a time of quietude before a soul proceeds further into the spirit world to engage with other spirits.

In Destiny of Souls under chapter four, spiritual energy restoration, I discuss the varieties of energy healing depending upon the condition of the returning soul. This list would include three general categories:

A. The standard treatment before orientation for large numbers of souls.
B. Emergency treatment for souls whose energy has been damaged by a violent death.
C. Special treatment in recovery areas designed for souls who have been severely contaminated throughout an entire lifetime.

I want to emphasize the fact that your client is not going to be disposed to giving you many details about their recovery areas after a tormented life. Unless I feel there is direct relevance today, I don't push them to do so because this experience is not something they must relive and dwell on to make our session a success. My therapeutic philosophy here is the same as I have expressed earlier under Desensitizing Trauma.

Perhaps blocked memories of energy restoration and recovery after former lives involves protective amnesia by our guides. On rare occasions when I do hear about radically damaged souls, these reports are often given to me by third parties who knew such souls or by a specialist soul in rehabilitation training. Drastic remodeling, or reshaping of soul energy from a badly contaminated spirit, may result in the soul never returning to Earth again. If a severe remodeling procedure was ever used on your client after a former life, it is being blocked as an act of kindness. I think it is best not to interfere.

30

Orientation with Guides

Since almost all your cases will involve some sort of orientation with a guide, you should be aware of the diverse aspects of this primary stop in the spirit world. I have spoken about the profound sense of awe your client feels in hypnosis at their first visual contact with their guide. These feelings become more verbal when the soul moves from the gateway with their guide to a space where acclimatization and past life review take place.

I think it would be helpful for the LBL therapist to reexamine what I have to say about orientation and guides comprising chapters five and eight in Journey of Souls. I discuss such matters as spiritual settings and the roles of senior and junior guides. This data will be pertinent to many of your cases. While the nuances of each case are different, you will find many similarities. For instance, at the initial contact with their guide, a devout Christian client might exclaim, "Oh, I see Jesus!" A variation of this theme could be a statement to the effect of "An angel has just come to meet me."

There are clients with firm theological convictions who tend to believe their session is a religious rather than a spiritual experience. Thus, conscious preconceptions toward religious doctrine are manifested here. I try to be careful with the sensibilities of clients in this regard and generally say, "That's fine, but let's get a little closer so we can have a better look at this figure." They soon realize this preeminent being is their own personal teacher who has been assigned to them from their beginnings rather than a great prophet from one of the world's major religions.

It is no wonder some people call personal guides "guardian angels." These floating beings don't have wings but sometimes the halo of bright white light around them gives this impression. Once your clients are on their way to an orientation, many will report that their guides wear robes and display a head with distinctive facial features and gender characteristics they did not see before.

The place of orientation is usually designed around some sort of comfortable and familiar Earth setting. Quite often my subjects report being in a garden where they are sitting on a white marble bench talking to their teacher. This setting could also be in a familiar room of some sort with a table and chairs, an area of open ground, or even an airy place composed of clouds.

You have already reviewed the client's most immediate past life and are aware of the circumstances surrounding goals that were and were not achieved. Thus, you may be able to assist with their memories of assimilation back into the spirit world. Orientation is a place of mental healing and it is possible you can learn much about your subject's current attitudes and conflicts in life by gently acting as a third party in these discussions between a soul and their guide. I will review how you can use the spirit world's now time reality as current therapy later in this text.

The following is a series of questions I typically pose to clients during orientation that may prove useful:

1. While you are talking to your guide, do you review what goals you established in advance of your past life? If so, how many of these goals were met?
2. Relative to these goals, could you tell me what was your greatest achievement and greatest disappointment in your past life?
3. How would you compare your last few lives with all those you lived before in terms of your continuing development?
4. Tell me about your guide's role in helping you before, during, and after your lives?

5. Does your guide offer any opinions about your overall advancement during this orientation?
6. What advice are you being given at this stage of your journey home?
7. Can you explain what other matters of importance to you transpire at this conference?

Orientation is a time when clients begin to gain deeper insights about themselves. Thus it is a good idea to try and relate your questions to what is going on in their current life. You will find that in these spiritual surroundings souls are quite honest about their shortcomings. Self-criticism runs high during orientation after a life is completed. While guides have differing styles, I find most operate around the premise, "Don't be so hard on yourself, you did very well."

As someone who has listened to thousands of guide-directed orientations, I can tell you they are never rigid or controlling. You will have the overall sense of empathic listening from guides because they already know everything about their soul client. Nothing can be hidden and the soul knows this absolutely. It is my belief that guides are assigned to each soul because they have some particular affinity toward the strengths and weaknesses in the immortal character of that soul. It is almost as if the teacher's character is similar to their student, or that they struggled at one time with the same tasks.

The love our guides feel for us is overpowering and during our lives often what we think is intuition or instinct is actually our guide trying to tell us something. After an LBL session, your client may explain that they now realize certain symbolic messages were left for them in earlier stages of their life to bring greater personal awareness and get them in focus. It is true that all guides are different. Some appear to be hands-on teachers who mentally assist us out of the deep holes we fall into during life while others are more distant in their approach and seem to be removed from our lives unless we call on them out of desperation in a crisis.

While your client talks about being frustrated at not accomplishing what they set out to do in their immediate past life, you may see the relationship to certain challenges in their current life. I try to concentrate on gaining broad information about the soul I am working with at this stage rather than focusing on too many specifics. From what I have discovered, orientation is not supposed to be an intense period of soul questioning by a guide but rather a gentle counseling and debriefing session. The deeper analysis involving the soul's perceptions and behavior in the life just completed normally becomes more evident later on in the spirit world.

There are periods during a long LBL session when your persistence in questioning the client is advantageous, but the time of orientation is not one of them. If your encouragement to elicit more facts is not productive, be aware that the most meaningful period for psychotherapy is usually when you take your client before their council. Of course, there is always the issue of privacy and feelings by some clients that they should not be revealing sacred aspects of their soul experience. It is peculiar, but I see more manifestations of a guarded attitude during orientation than I do at other junctures in the LBL session. Over the years, I have come to some conclusions about this phenomenon.

It is true that orientation is the first one-on-one opportunity for the soul to unload their impressions about the last incarnation with a teacher. However, some souls may not be completely ready just yet because they need to unwind. There are other factors that might cause a client to be reticent about speaking freely at this stage. Aside from privacy issues, I think it has more to do with a lack of full comprehension.

Since the orientation stop is early in their progression into the spirit world after death, the soul still has strong attachments to the organic body they have just left. Vestiges of their biological temperament and personality from that body do remain for a while after a life. This happens despite the fact the newly arrived soul is now in possession of their immortal character. Because of these factors, soul memories from orientation may initially cause even more confusion in the mind of a client reporting to you from a whole new biological state, that of their current body.

It takes a while to work through the transformation your client will experience into a deeper, more pure soul state between lives. As the session progresses you will see that the whole psychological reality of spiritual life becomes more literal and graphic for the subject. If you are patient with your therapeutic approaches during orientation, it will pay dividends later when your subjects fully see themselves as spiritual beings.

Since orientation is intended to be an overview for the returning soul, often spirit time may seem rather short to them. Clients frequently say they don't remember all the details about their last orientation, and perhaps they are not supposed to remember too much of this experience in their current body. Thus, for many reasons, the average client will not mind your desire to get them moving on to the next station when orientation information dries up. At the appropriate moment I ask:

> Is it time to move to your next stop?

With an inadequate response I might be more specific:

> Do you think it is time to rejoin your friends?

Usually, the answer is yes.

As hypnosis facilitators, we do exert a great deal of control over the design and pace of a session. In fact, your subject unconsciously seeks your direction. However, I must warn you that your clients will have preferences for some spiritual images over others. For therapeutic reasons, I may feel at a particular point in the session I should ask:

> For your own mental well-being, is there a particular place where you want us to move right now in the spirit world that would be of great benefit?

They may or may not agree to follow your suggestion. Just because you think a certain spiritual scene is appropriate to introduce at the moment does not mean that your subject will concur. They might want to visit other areas of the spirit world first before going someplace you suggest. Moreover, there are clients who will not visualize the same spiritual scenes that are typical of the majority of your other clients. Always use the subject's own directional compass when it is intact. Your clients may wish to revisit places in their spiritual memory that directly bear upon what they require today and will be able to guide you, rather than the reverse. If you encounter any resistance to move at a certain stage in spiritual regression, you might simply ask:

> Is there more you want to continue examining at the moment, or are you ready to travel with me to another area?

Always be flexible and open in your planning, while encouraging constant feedback. Be prepared for a great deal of silence from your subject while they are mentally processing. I believe that people receive quantities of spiritual information that is not revealed to you by the spoken word. After a certain amount of effort on your part you must accept these gaps. They will be quite evident on the audio tapes during replaying. An LBL session is truly a client-therapist partnership. The longer you work in this field, the more you will feel spiritually guided toward the best course of action.

As I have said, for some souls the period right after orientation may be an appropriate time for reflection, solitude, or a visit to the spiritual library for private study. After a difficult life, soul healing often occurs in quiet places, away from groups of companion souls and even our spiritual masters. In Destiny of Souls, I have gone into considerable detail about the library of life books. If your client indicates they are going to some sort of spiritual library in response to an inquiry involving solitude or study, I suggest the following series of questions:

1. Are you conducted to the library by your guide, or do you go alone?
2. How does this area of study appear to you during your approach?
3. Describe your entry into this space and tell me if you see other souls nearby.
4. Is there an advanced spiritual being (such as an archivist) in charge of this area?
5. Tell me what you see around you at this moment.
6. Do you feel this is going to be a time of life review?
7. Will you be reading something written in a book, looking at still pictures, or viewing a movie screen of some sort?
8. Now, begin your work and tell me if you find yourself reading, or watching pictures as an observer, or do you enter into a scene to actually participate in past events?
9. What are you learning or experiencing that relates to your current life?

As you and your client move from place to place in the spirit world, it is always wise to suggest that they call upon their guide to assist with directions and the rate of soul transition. With an indecisive client, rather than directing the client to another stop of your choosing too quickly, perhaps the client just needs to hear "What is it you want to do at this particular moment?"

Part Five
LIFE BETWEEN LIVES

31

Returning Clients to Their Soul Group

This last stop for the average incoming soul is particularly enjoyable. Through hypnosis, the client is given the opportunity to visit those soul companions who are close to them. Synchronicity always plays a part in LBL hypnotherapy. The client may need to have contact with a particular soul at the time of their session with you. After the incoming soul's first sighting of their friends, who are gathered in some sort of cluster grouping, I find guides make themselves scarce. They seem to be hovering nearby at this stage and yet many people report that they are going in solo, even during the last portions of this journey. Nevertheless, souls do not express discomfort or feel abandoned by their guides.

During the final stages of the trip home, you must be prepared for a variety of reports from different clients. Some subjects will describe beautiful open fields and countryside settings where their companions are waiting. Others see structures such as temples, libraries, or schoolhouses. Transitions to these places vary between clients and between their lives. In Journey of Souls, chapter six, under transition, I describe the memories of souls who reported traveling toward great central hubs of activity before moving into more quiet zones where they saw transparent bubbles containing clusters of souls off in the distance.

In Destiny of Souls, chapter five, under community centers, I wrote about a common visual occurrence with clients who see a great recreational hall full of soul groups, one of which belongs to the incoming soul. Chapter five has case descriptions about this meeting hall composed of secondary groups of up to a thousand souls. The client's primary group in the hall averages from ten to twenty souls (figure 1, reproduced in this appendix).

Why is it that some clients find their soulmates in open countryside scenes as opposed to spaces involving a structure of some sort? Why do some incoming souls see many soul groups conversing together in community halls while others are aware of only a few friends gathered to meet them? This is not something we can know absolutely, but over many years I have drawn some conclusions. We might logically begin by assuming that the time of departure from Earth right after death would influence a soul's point of reentry into a continuing sequence of spiritual activities. I do know that the same souls can have different reentry experiences after each past life.

A more subtle meaning pertaining to different visualizations of spiritual settings at reentry could have a symbolic relationship to the life just completed. They may directly relate to character traits of the soul as well as the temporary personality acquired in the life just lived. The question you must ask yourself is, "What is it that this soul requires most to integrate back into the spirit world?" A therapist should consider both the personal identity and life history of their client. There is also the issue of what current beliefs are held by your client that might be influencing their visualizations. The soul's developmental level ought to be taken into account as well.

When I examine the symbolic significance of certain scenes, I can say that souls who have just crossed over will relate their earthly experiences in the life just completed to spiritual encounters that seem familiar. I believe that metaphorical comparisons, in which an idea or picture is applied to offer a certain meaning, can even be orchestrated by guides. When the mind is trying to process interpretations of spiritual images it may construct metaphors to make the information more palatable to physical reality. Regardless of the arrival surroundings, always consider what function the scene represents to the soul. Here are some examples:

A. Gardens represent spaces of security and peace combined with gentle counseling by guides.
B. Temples (including community halls) represent spaces of spiritual communion with others.
C. Schoolhouses and classrooms represent areas associated with soul group learning exercises and teachers.
D. Libraries are quiet spaces designed for personal study and individual reflection.
E. Primary soul group enclosures are places the incoming soul associates with the privacy of a home and family interaction.

Sooner or later in the session, but most commonly right after orientation, the time will be suitable for you to bring your client forward to the space where they are able to see all their soul companions. They could take you there without prompting or you might have to ask:

Is it time to rejoin your friends?

Usually, you will hear soul group descriptions that indicate a kind of space within a space where these soul companions are gathered. This area (not in a recreational hall) is considered a spiritual haven. Particularly with the younger souls, a transparent enclosure may actually represent a boundary separate from other cluster groups.

Throughout this stage of connecting with members of their soul groups, clients respond well to questions about feeling certain soul vibrational levels. The individual and collective vibrational frequency of companion souls increases as the client approaches their soul group, where there are mutual feelings of joyous expectation.

32

Identification of Soulmates

Before going further with soul identification within a cluster group, it is a good idea to recognize the three major categories of souls in our immortal lives:

A. Primary soulmates: Frequently, but not always, this soul is a deeply bonded partner, such as a spouse. This soul could also be a brother, sister, best friend, and even a parent on rare occasions.
B. Companion soulmates: These are the souls within a cluster group who make up our spiritual family. Normally, these souls are siblings, children, and good friends as participants in our physical life.
C. Affiliated souls: These are all the souls who make up secondary groups of souls located around our own primary cluster. They often incarnate as parents as well as protagonists to teach us certain karmic lessons. Typically, they are acquaintances in life who are associated with us for a reason. However, many of the souls in nearby groups are unknown to us both in life and the spirit world.

There are practical variations within these three general categories of souls. For instance, it is quite possible for a client to have only a brief association with a soul in life who is actually a soul companion in their soul group and not an affiliated soul. The reasons for this may have karmic significance relating to a former life.

Identification of Soulmates | 121

As you bring your subject closer to the area where they see the light energy forms of a soul gathering, their responses often become rather halting. Under the topic of pacing, I have mentioned the importance of moving slowly at certain periods in the session. Soul identification is one of those intervals where you must allow your client plenty of time to respond to questions. When a subject says to me, "I'm coming from a distance away and I can't make out what I am seeing," my acknowledgement would be:

> You are doing fine; take your time and move closer. Just be patient and everything will soon come into focus for you.

As your client draws closer, they will say something to the effect of, "I see points of lights together." These visualizations are similar to their reports about lights during the crossing phase of the session. I generally respond with three basic questions:

1. Tell me what you see them doing.

A standard reply would be, "I think they are waiting for me." My next question is one requiring a closer examination:

2. How are they arranged in front of you?

If the client does not respond or is unsure, I will follow up with a few choices:

3. Do you see these lights moving about singly, in pairs, or as one large cluster of brightness?

Bringing subjects close to their soul group is also described in Destiny of Souls under chapter five, detailing two of the most common cluster group positions (figures 2 and 3, reproduced in this appendix): the phalanx-diamond and the half-circle position. Notice the positions of the returning soul in relation to their guide, who is behind them in these illustrations. As I have said, in most instances your client's guide will not be next to the incoming soul. I have indicated that during this entire phase of returning souls to their groups, most guides tend to remain unobtrusive.

In fact, souls don't seem to have the need to converse with their guides at all at this stage. Once the soul moves close to their cluster group during the recognition phase, many clients are only vaguely aware their guides are positioned somewhere around them. In other cases, you could have clients who recognize their guide standing in back or well to the side of a line of souls during the identification of individual cluster group members. You will realize this situation from those clients who remark, "One light is brighter and a different color from the rest."

I think it would be helpful to offer a case example of my clock technique, which I find useful for soul group identification. The client in this case is named Susan. She is visualizing herself as a returning soul who has just encountered a semicircle of lights she knows are friends.

Dr. N: As you move close to the lights of your friends, I want you to tell me how they are arranged in front of you—in a line, a circle, a half-circle, or bunched up?

Susan: Ah . . . in a kind of half-circle.

Dr. N: Good. Now count how many lights you see. Take your time and tell me how many there are.

Susan: (pause) Oh . . . I see . . . nine.

Dr. N: And as you come toward them, are you positioned in the center, on the left, or on the right of these nine lights?

Susan: (more confidently) In the center.

Dr. N: Okay, now, in order to help me, just imagine that all these souls are located around you like the numbers on the face of a clock. You are in the center, where the hands of the clock would be placed. Thus, the light directly in front of you is at twelve o'clock, the one on your far left is at nine o'clock, and the light on your far right is at three o'clock. As you draw closer, if a light should move behind you, it would be at six o'clock. The rest of your friends can be anywhere in between. Do you understand?

Susan: Yes.

Dr. N: Good. Now tell me from what position on our clock does the first soul move toward you?

Susan: Oh ... in front—at twelve o'clock.

Dr. N: Is this being a male- or female-appearing figure?
Susan: Male.
Dr. N: Who is this person in the life you just left?
Susan: My husband, Jim.

Note: If this is an emotional reunion, I will stop to give my client time to embrace this person and report whatever she wishes about the communication between them.

Dr. N: And who is this person in your life today?
Susan: My God! It's my husband, Bill.
Dr. N: What is Bill's immortal spiritual name?
Susan: Sha ... ah ... Shamo ...
Dr. N: And what is your own immortal name? What does Shamo call you?

Note: You may have already asked for your client's spirit name earlier in the session, but if you have not done so, or you were unsuccessful, this is an opportune time to learn the name.

Susan: Lila ... I am called Lila.

Dr. N: All right, Lila, what color does Shamo project to you?

Susan: Mmm ... yellow and white.

Dr. N: If I were standing where Shamo is now—and holding up a full-length mirror toward you—what colors would you be radiating?

Susan: The same colors.

By using soul names as early as possible in the session, you establish greater personal identification between the client and their soul. Also, they feel more connected with the action unfolding in their minds about the spirit world.

33

Recognition of Soul Colors

I could have asked Susan simply, "What light color do you project?" However, I have found that the use of a pictorial approach, where the soul sees themselves symbolically in a reflecting mirror, allows for a more objective response when reporting on their personal color. Moreover, since clients will be visualizing some sort of soul group configuration with many colors, this should be reinforced with the client and diagrammed in your notes. Usually, the client will see the positions of souls around them in a half-circle. It makes it much easier for the client to see or feel their companions if you move around the circle, identifying each member of the group by name, color, and personal characteristics. If the souls are bunched up or in a diamond shape, you would simply identify those in front first and then move backward.

In figure 4 of the appendix, I list the color spectrum of spiritual auras associated with observable levels of souls. The generally accepted meaning of these soul colors based on countless client reports appears in Destiny of Souls under soul group systems. In figure 5 of the appendix, I offer an example of the energy colors displayed by a typical soul group composed of eleven souls. Current relatives and friends from this soul group in the subject's life today are also identified.

Under the section in this text's First Contact with Spirits (Part Four), I mentioned that colors are generated by the specific energy vibrations of each soul. Souls display halo and core colors. The primary core color emanating from the center of the soul-being constitutes the level of soul advancement, while the secondary color around the edges of the light, the halo, typically involves character traits. Core and halo colors may be different or the same. You might have a Level II reddish-orange soul whose character represents intensity and passion. This soul would show one color. To give other illustrations of character, yellow is typically a persevering color of strength and courage, while green denotes healing, blue knowledge, and purple wisdom.

With soul energy, one must be careful not to confuse client reports of bright gold colors with the basic yellow tones. Many Level III souls have a primary yellow color, which is often less vivid than bright gold. Highly advanced souls may display brilliant, glittering gold, frequently as flecks mixed with the blues and purples. Gold presents a highly refined energy pattern and yet it does represent similar characteristics to yellow in terms of protective strength and influence toward other, less advanced souls. It is a very powerful, active color.

Because the light and dark blues and purples represent more advanced souls, I am frequently asked, "What is the difference between knowledge and wisdom?" The blues are mental and analytical souls who are very devoted to the details of cause and effect with regard to karma. Some blues are more detached in the realm of the spirit world and are committed to interdimensional travel. In this case, the blue is the level of advancement and may be mixed with silver, an ethereal color associated more with the individual nature of the soul.

As for the highly evolved darker purple colors displayed by very senior guides and council members, we find knowledge that has transcended into wisdom that is broad and eclectic in scope linked to experience and talent. All indications point to our council members as being responsible for our next body and thus they must apply great wisdom and originality in problem solving. The matching of soul character to a human brain is ingenious—or perhaps I should say divine. Certainly, both the darker blue and purple beings are highly principled, decisive, and organizational, yet they display great creativity and have infinite patience, forgiveness, and love.

As an LBL facilitator, it is best to be cautious about inflexible rules connected with the meaning of soul colors. I have found that a very high percentage of clients agree that certain attributes do apply to particular colors and to the developmental stage of souls who display these colors. Even so, there are always exceptions because energy vibrations are subtle and anomalies do occur. Moreover, we cannot always trust every client observer to be consistent with all the details in their accounts throughout the session. For the facilitator, it is prudent not to jump to conclusions about colors too quickly before cross-checking all your client reports.

As I move my client around their group, I make notes of each soul position and ask:

> What color do you see radiating from this soul?

Even though a soul is displaying more than one color during the group visualizations, the subject may just lump both into one dominant color without more serious consideration. More often than not, if only one central color is seen, especially from a distance, it usually represents the level of advancement. I also keep a record of the luminosity of each light. Does the soul display a steady, brilliant light of a high-energy soul, or is it dim and flickering, indicting a more passive or younger soul? These reports provide clues to a soul's attributes.

34

Gathering Information on a Soul Group

Collecting information on each soul member takes time because many subjects identify their soul companions slowly. You owe it to your client to give them all the time they require so no cluster group member is missed. This is why taking detailed notes is important. I start taking notes in the session from the moment we enter the client's past life so I can always refer back to their previous statements for corroboration. As an example, I might comment, "When we approached your cluster group, you told me there were ten souls, but now you only mentioned nine. Are we missing one soul?" If necessary, I will go further by adding, "I notice there are souls at two and four o'clock; is someone at three?"

It is very handy to have the client's typed sheet listing the cast of characters in their current life in front of you during this stage. Hopefully, your notes written down during intake about the social dynamics between family members will also be useful. As the client identifies each soul companion, usually there are two names, their Earth name and the immortal name. As with the names of guides, sometimes the spiritual name can be difficult to pronounce. While the subject sounds out the name, just as I instructed them to do earlier with their guide, I ask them to also try and spell the names of each companion, which I then write down. If it is incomplete, I will say, "I'll just use what we have now. You can correct me if necessary as we go along."

Corrections often come a short while later, after the client has heard me mispronounce the name a few times. This works particularly well with your subject's own immortal name.

35

Primary Soulmates

As your subject begins to identify each member of their soul group, invariably you will witness a highly emotional scene when they sight their primary soulmate. Frequently this particular being is their first identification because it is common for a primary soul to come forward before anyone else. My previous books contain much information about soulmates. For purposes of this text, I want to touch on one therapeutic issue involving soulmates that can be most disturbing to your client should it arise at this point in the session.

Anyone who has experienced a relationship with a great love in their life knows that the chemistry of a mental and physical reunion is capable of transforming the spirit. The essence of this conjoining energy is feeling that all at once part of yourself resides in another. Soulmates who are together make each other more complete with mutual validation. When it is right, the togetherness of true love transforms the old self into a stronger force than before. Incarnating to express themselves in physical form is one of the basic motivations for primary soulmates to come to Earth and meet. People worry that following the "wrong" person in life may cause them to miss their star. Nevertheless, this too is no accident.

When your client visualizes coming together with their primary soulmate in the spirit world, it is one of the most joyful moments in their session with you. Even so, I want you to be prepared for those clients who will state in a depressed tone,

"My soulmate is not with me in my current life." Perhaps they were never intended to be in this life or maybe this person was an earlier love they lost. In these circumstances, only at best is your client's first reaction one of understanding and acceptance.

More often than not, the client's initial impression is that they have been cheated. This is due to negative feedback from the conscious mind. Despite being in a superconscious state, a client in this frame of mind is suddenly overcome by feelings of a loss of support. They blame a less than satisfying life on the fact their primary soulmate is absent. Naturally, the impact here is even greater with the realization of how many past lives they have lived together. These memories are more potent when the client has already relived a past life earlier in the session where they were mated to their primary soulmate.

All souls have the power of choice in their lives because without free will our lessons would mean nothing. During an LBL session, while a client is emotionally rebonding with a primary soulmate who is not in their life today, I indicate that behind this absence lies some aspect of learning which they have chosen in advance. I want my client to process this information for themselves because self-discovery is always the best teaching tool. It is vital to listen and not get ahead of your client with your own interpretations while they are unraveling the meaning behind events. I gently remind clients that free will comes with a price, which is the right to make mistakes—and this is how we learn.

When people ask me at public forums why they have never found their soulmate in life, I explain they may have done so but for many reasons an opportunity might have been missed. I add that it is also possible they were not intended to be with their primary soulmate this time around. To illustrate this, I will cite the case of Catherine, who came to see me with the question, "Why can't I find my true love?"

Catherine has had a difficult current life with poor relationships, starting with emotionally distant parents, two husbands who were not connected with her, and a series of men who did not work out for various reasons. Today she lives with an emotionally protective man who is also her business partner. They care for each other but are not in love. During Catherine's session we learned this man is a strong member of their soul group but is not her primary soulmate. The two souls agreed to come together around the middle of their respective lives and work with each other.

In Catherine's last life, she had a long, happy marriage with her primary soulmate from 1874 to 1927 in Savannah. They were inseparable for over fifty years, dying within a year of each other. It was a beautiful, quiet, and restful life without many outside challenges because they were given what is called a "by" in that life due to two difficult previous lives where they were not together. Both asked for an easy life with each other and then received it. Catherine gained perspective into her life today when she discovered that after thousands of years of often being together with her primary soulmate (not always as a spouse), they had become too dependent upon one another and shut out other people. To work harder in meeting the challenges of life and advancing, they needed to be apart more often.

When working with a client who is saddened because they are not with their primary soulmate, I think the LBL therapist should make it clear that people can have productive and enriching relationships with men and women who are not soulmates. I have found close, loving alliances do exist among companion souls from the same cluster group and also with souls from affiliated groups. They are working together for some mutually beneficial karmic purpose. When your client discovers all this was planned in advance it eases the burden they feel to keep searching for the right person.

I have a standard question to ask those clients who say they are with the wrong person or spent years with a very difficult or abusive individual earlier in life:

> What have you learned from this person that you would not otherwise have known had you never met them?

I want to know if they are stronger and wiser for the experience. We are with people in life who have something to teach us, just as we do for them. The lessons are countless, involving such issues as jealously, greed, arrogance, intolerance, and lack of compassion. Karma rests on our actions over the sum of many lives, not just one. For these lessons, our primary soulmate may assume the role of a blood relative or best friend. Sometimes your client may find that they have been in a love relationship with a primary soulmate for only a short time to learn one specific lesson before being separated. Hopefully, this aspect of your client's LBL session will allow them to come away with a better appreciation for the reasons behind their experiences. By the end of the session most clients realize that life is not just a capricious jumble of unrelated events.

36

The Inner Circle and Missing Soul Companions

As therapists, we must be mindful of interpersonal connections in the lives of clients with those people around them. Spiritual regression increases a client's perceptions about the meaning of having certain soul companions affect their lives, both positively and negatively. While you are working with your client in the identification of soul companions in a cluster group, you will be exposed to an "inner circle." This designation is used to describe a smaller group of intimate companion souls who often incarnate as spouses, brothers, sisters, and best friends. They may also be aunts, uncles, and cousins. It is possible to find a parent but this is uncommon because frequently our parents come from nearby affiliated groups. An inner circle usually consists of three to five souls who invariably assume lifetime roles close to each other.

Sometimes prospective clients will ask you to schedule back-to-back sessions with themselves and their mates, siblings, and best friends. The keeping of detailed records is particularly valuable when two clients who know each other wish to compare their LBL sessions. It is true they have their tape recordings, but you will have made additional notes to yourself that are not on these audio recordings. Having your prior notes from the first client near you during a later session with a spouse, sibling, or friend is useful in asking relevant questions. These notes are confidential and for your use only.

Regardless of the length of time between the two sessions, there will be occasions when one of these pairs of people sees a member of their inner circle and the other does not. This could cause distress, especially to a happily married couple. For instance, if Jane sees her husband, John, in her spirit group but John does not see Jane when it is his turn, does that invalidate Jane's visualization? My answer is no, it does not. We might argue that possibly John's soul is more significant in Jane's life than the reverse, but in most cases this, too, is a wrong assumption.

I believe that there are three major grounds for a disparity between hypnosis visualizations of two souls from the same group who are bonded in life:

A. The timing of arrival into the group from a former life between the two souls is different.

Using Jane and John as an example, when pressed further John might say, "I don't see Jane right now because she is away and engaged in an activity, but I feel her presence."

B. One soul may not wish to show themselves right away to another because of a difficult karmic issue between them in their last life together.

I call this the "hunkering-down syndrome," where one soul hides behind another during the group identification process until a more appropriate period. In Destiny of Souls, chapter seven, case forty-seven, I have a section on reuniting souls who have hurt each other. This involves a father and son case that characterizes this situation. Remember that it does not matter if the soul of a parent has reincarnated again years before the arrival of their child in the spirit world, because a portion of their energy never left. Generational differences do not affect spiritual reunions because of this capacity for soul division.

C. The differences between visualizations by two clients may be due to the nature of remaining energy from the effects of soul division.

37

Soul Energy

In the context of relationships between clients that are closely bonded with others on Earth who they want to see in the spirit world, the issue of soul division involving incarnated energy is an element to consider. In the example of John and Jane I just discussed, John may not see Jane because Jane displays only a faint light from her remaining energy in the spirit world. If a soul companion is not clear or is unseen during the initial soul group identification, it may be due to their "dim light dormancy," a term used by subjects to explain a low percentage of rather inactive energy. The reasons for this could be that the soul required a great deal of their energy for a particularly difficult reincarnation—say 80 percent—so what light remains is faint. Dim light (not to be confused with younger souls) is particularly evident with souls who have chosen to live parallel lives in two bodies in the same timeline. This practice, designed to accelerate learning, is not encouraged by guides for the average soul because it causes such an energy drain.

On the other hand, I have had clients that are not living parallel lives who decided to bring less energy (under 30 percent) into a host body because they were overconfident about their capacity to handle a life. Many of these clients felt a lack of energy in life without knowing why. Their motivations were to leave a greater percentage of energy in the spirit world to carry on their work there more vigorously. This remaining energy would thus appear brighter in the spirit world. There are people who make themselves less effective on Earth because of this decision. The average soul takes around 50 to 70 percent of their energy into a body. This can vary from life to life, depending on a soul's body choices and state of advancement. What would happen if a soul were permitted to bring too much energy into a body? One client answered that question in this way: "Too much incarnated energy, like in the 90+ percent range, would overload the brain, making it nonfunctional—100 percent would blow the circuits."

In terms of soul division, I should add it appears that once a decision is made to take a given amount of energy to Earth, souls are not able to retrieve more during their lifetime, regardless of how much they may need it. Besides the potential for human brain disruptions from a new and permanent energy surge, I don't think it would be physically possible for the human brain to tolerate a lasting transfer of new energy. It has been said that we are able to tap into our entire spiritual energy during times of stress through prayer or meditation. When an LBL facilitator assists the client in connecting with all their energy in a superconscious state, it may seem as though there is a transfusion of new energy. You will notice a reaction of energy unification with some clients as they experience an awareness of their whole being. However, I have often been told that while in a physical body the soul-mind cannot simply withdraw from its reserves of energy in the spirit world and keep it. We live by our choices made between lives just as we do during our incarnations; it is like being under a contract. The following perspective about connecting with his spiritual energy reserve came to me from Evan, a Level V soul:

> There is a directly proportional relationship between my brain and the energy of my soul. This was established in the womb. It is true I can temporarily draw upon the energy I left in the spirit world if my energy has been depleted

during a crisis. I can also work in reverse, sending portions of my energy from the spirit world into my body. This rejuvenation can occur during sleep or if my body is under anesthetic or in a coma. The restriction which does exist is that energy boosting cannot be permanent or it would adversely alter my brain waves into an unfamiliar state of being. At the least, it would create a personality disorder. At worst, insanity.

Because I wish to know the delicate balance that exists between the energy of the soul and the brain, I often ask my clients questions about their incarnated energy:

1. What percentage of your total energy did you bring into your current body?
2. Do you think you brought enough to complete the goals you established for your body?
3. Are you able to tap into that portion of your energy which remains in the spirit world on a temporary basis from Earth?

As an LBL facilitator, you have the opportunity to encourage clients to be more aware of their internal energy resources during times of emotional turmoil in life.

38

Examining Character Types in Groups

During your examination of a cluster group there are standard questions that you will ask of all clients. Here are a few examples:

1. Of all the souls you see, who is in your life today?
2. Of the souls you have identified, who are the ones you have most often incarnated with in your past lives and why?
3. Starting with your primary soulmate, tell me the significant roles certain souls in your group most enjoy filling.
4. Identify the different character types within your inner circle of closest friends.
5. In your opinion, what is the general state of advancement of your group? Are you all advancing at about the same rate?

Once the identification of souls in a primary group is completed, I may ask a couple of open-ended questions, such as:

6. What thoughts are you receiving from your group?
7. Is there anything meaningful going on right now between you and your group that you can tell me about?

Perhaps there is a planned homecoming celebration or some other activity that I might miss if I did not allow the subject to fully explore their visualization of this scene. It is possible the client will open up new territory with, "I think I must go now to another place." This could mean a visit to their council for a life review, going to the library for study, participating in a classroom exercise, or engaging in some sort of recreational activity. If this happens, you will just have to follow your client's inclinations and bring them back to their group later if your investigations here are unfinished.

If there is no urgency in leaving their cluster group, you could start a new line of inquiry along the following lines:
8. If I was a visitor to your group, what impression would I take away about all of you?
9. Why do you think you were all brought together to form this group in the beginning?
10. Is there a common denominator of talent, interest, and goals among you? Do you all aspire to specialize in the same area? (Of course they don't, but this could generate an intriguing answer.)

Your client could start anywhere, with such responses as, "A lot of us are healers. Most of us want to be teachers. We are pleasure-oriented and not very studious." These reports lead to other questions that will tell you more about the characteristics of your subject's immortal soul and how this being integrates with others in their group. Most groups do have certain common dispositions that bind them together because you can be sure there were reasons why a primary group was formed with these particular souls. In Journey of Souls, chapter seven, I refer to the homogeneous aspects of a group's members, such as mutual interests and cognitive awareness. I hear that most souls in a cluster group seem to grow at about the same rate but you are going to find there are the slower ones who will be the last to leave.

However, be aware that most groups of companion souls are actually designed to have a mix of character differences. I outline this dichotomy in chapter nine of Journey of Souls. For instance, there are the courageous, tenacious survivors; quiet, more passive souls; calculating souls; and fun-loving, humorous souls. This system is planned so that each soul is capable of supporting others in their group during a lifetime. Each soul in the group lends its strength to another's shortcomings for balance. For example, on Earth you could have two soulmates working together where the husband is overanalytical and cautious while his wife is more emotional and a risk taker. Due in part to the bodies they occupy and in part to the soul energy of those bodies, the two souls complement one another.

By comparing the character traits of your client's soul to the rest of the souls in their group, you help them understand what is behind the attitudes and social dynamics of their relationships with significant people in their lives today. It would also be advisable to check this information against the vibrational energy colors of individual members of the group for further contrasts. Collecting all this color data, including client reports about light density, provides you with further clues about the group regarding character, current relationships, and individual rates of growth, all of which can be of therapeutic value to your client.

As you explore the cluster group, you will find a senior master teacher and quite often a junior guide or student teacher in training. They may be identified by your client right away, or this information may come from a question:

> Do you see someone in the vicinity directing your group?

Frequently, a junior guide is left in charge while a senior guide is away. This being may still be incarnating from time to time, but nonetheless is still a teacher.

As I mentioned earlier, you will have cases when after a former life your subject enters the spirit world and right away rejoins their friends in the middle of a classroom situation. I am always interested in group classroom assignments, such as energy creation training. The level of these assignments will also give you clues about the group's abilities and goals. It is possible the class will be involved with a psychodrama of certain past life performances by its members. This activity is instructive about the group's capabilities. I will review psychodrama by a group of souls further in Part Five regarding other spirit-world activities.

I have stated in my books that despite all the differences between souls, no soul is looked down upon as having less value because they are not progressing as fast as others in the group. Everyone makes contributions and all are in a process of transition. There are souls who want every life to be difficult, while others prefer many easy lives mixed into the lives involving greater effort. We are given choices. Because there is order and direction in the spirit world, where accomplishment is venerated, this does not mean the afterlife is a place of hierarchy with a rigid set of bureaucratic rules. Those are the trappings of our earthly societies. Souls are not forced to reincarnate at regular intervals and live demanding lives. Before each life there are options and souls feel no authoritarian pressure to succeed within certain earthly time frames. The desire to grow and develop in life after life comes from within ourselves.

After you have finished your more specific questions about their primary group, I suggest you broaden your inquiries to include nearby groups. Of course, much depends on the level of responsiveness from the client up to this stage. If I am getting good results, I might continue with this question:

> Now that I know of the many character differences between your soul companions, can you tell me if you are aware of a soul existing nearby in another group whose character is very similar to your own and at about the same level of development?

Certainly, you will draw blanks from many clients with this sort of question, but once in a while you will uncover a gem of information. I once had a client, Laura, who was in a current life that was designed around the probability she would lose her second son, Jason (age eighteen), in a drowning accident. Jason's soul was a member of Laura's primary soul group, a companion soul who was very close to her. This soul volunteered to live only eighteen years (if such indications were realized) because that allotment of time was enough for Jason to complete certain tasks and fulfill a karmic lesson for Laura.

During the process of Laura's life selection it was decided that she needed a lifetime of emotional support from a strong soul whose immortal character was much like her own. A kindred spirit was chosen from a secondary group some distance away from her primary group. This affiliated soul took the role of Laura's eldest son, Steve. While Steve and his mother had many battles in his teens because they were so much alike, he was there for Laura when Jason died and his father left the family as an outgrowth of all the trauma and grief. Laura's perceptions about the scheme of things and Steve's role were greatly enhanced by these revelations.

Below are samples of other questions about nearby affiliated soul groups you might consider:

1. What are your connections with souls from other groups in the same vicinity of your primary group?
2. Do you personally have any association with certain souls in another cluster group?
3. Are the other groups around you generally of a more advanced nature or are they less developed than your own group?
4. Could you tell me how the origin of your group compares with others in your general spatial area?
5. Do you know if your guide participates with guides of other groups for activities of mutual benefit between various groups?

39

Clients in the Intermediate and Advanced Levels

An absence of orientation is one of the first indications that your client has advanced beyond their original group of souls. Another sign of soul advancement occurs at reentry when you ask them to identify lights in the distance. Under the section First Contact with Spirits (Part Four), I discussed elements of the color white pertaining to younger souls. Occasionally you will have a client who says, "I see a cluster of small, flickering white lights waiting for me"—this usually means one thing. You have a more advanced teaching soul who wishes to see their students before anyone else.

Typically, these lights represent very young souls who have not yet begun their incarnations and your client is one of their student teachers. Playful, humorous souls who are considered to be children souls often appear as small, dancing, white lights. These young souls display innocence and exuberance, and are easily distracted. Being a student teacher usually means the client is part of an independent study group of developing teachers who will someday be full-fledged guides.

However, if you have a more advanced client who is not a student teacher, they won't see the lights of younger souls waiting for them and there will be no need for deviation on the trip inward. The non-teacher advanced client will generally go directly to a space where they are able to rejoin peers in their independent study group. If any of your clients are rather new to this level of advancement, say Level III, there could be some initial confusion in their minds as to the whereabouts of their primary group. This is because they see none of their old soul companions, with the possible exception of one or two original friends.

Be aware that souls in transition to Level III may see both their primary group and a specialized independent study group. Discussing the character makeup of each of these groups will help you and your client differentiate one from another. Souls in primary groups at Levels I and II are made up of beings who have differences in talent, interest, and motivation toward certain activities. However, once a soul evolves into the intermediate and upper levels of knowledge, wisdom, and experience, they are often matched with like-minded souls from other primary cluster groups.

It is at Level III where specialization begins for souls in training for such activities as teachers, life-form designers, explorer souls, and library archivists. If your client is rather new to the intermediate levels they may be alternating their time about equally between the old and the new group. An independent study group, focusing on one skill, usually consists of far fewer souls than primary groups. Despite this, a rather new Level III might not recognize all their new colleagues right away. However, if your client has progressed into a solid Level IV, they should recognize the advanced souls with whom they work more quickly. I should add that advanced souls still maintain contact with their old primary soul companions during activity periods that do not involve specialization training.

For additional information regarding more advanced souls, I recommend a review of chapters ten and eleven in Journey of Souls, and chapter eight in Destiny of Souls. I have found with the more advanced souls that this stage in their session may be a good time to discuss just what they are studying before moving on to scenes with their council. This is an appropriate moment to consult with the advancing client about their aspirations, ideals, and goals as a spirit.

40

Taking Clients before Their Council

There are many open-ended questions that can be asked of the soul following a cluster group visit in terms of where to travel next. Depending on the degree of resistance, perhaps only the first or second question below will be necessary:

1. Where would you like us to go now?
2. Do you wish to stay with your cluster group and engage in some sort of activity with them?
3. Are you ready to move off to some specific kind of activity that is most important?

The last question is an open invitation to discuss the council. There are no firm spiritual rules of procedure connected to the timing of council visits. Following reentry, the average client will be ready to visit a collective of higher beings soon after returning to their cluster group. Even so, you must be prepared for alternatives to this normal pattern. Council meetings can come before or after group homecomings, time in solitary reflection, library study, or a classroom experience. The same client may have different council schedules, depending on the life just completed.

Be aware that you will have clients who seem somewhat disoriented by the sequence of spiritual events following life. I commented earlier about subjects who get bogged down at the gateway into the spirit world and require a little nudging to move forward. While the gateway is a particular trouble spot for client disorientation or even obstruction, confusion can happen anytime in the session. For instance, if your subject seems stuck right after visiting their primary group, I might say:

> Is anything confusing to you at the moment that you would like to tell me about?

If a long pause brings no results, my follow-up question would probably be more specific:

> Do you think this is an appropriate time for us to move to the space where you have the honor to appear before a group of wise beings who are waiting to help you?

Most people nod their head and say, "Yes." Indeed, by asking this question I know it looks as though I am shamelessly leading the client. From long experience, I have learned with some clients that some sort of encouragement is necessary at certain stages in the session. I believe my subjects see such prodding statements by me as an affirmation of their own knowledge and capacity to report about the spirit world. I have previously mentioned that gentle direction at appropriate times also gives the client confidence that you are a knowledgeable spiritual traveler.

A client may say, "No, I am not ready to see my council," or "I don't see myself going in front of a council." There could be a number of reasons for this kind of resistance. Usually this means that there were major karmic problems in the last life. The best plan for the LBL facilitator is to simply be encouraging without forcing the issue. Another reason for a client not wanting to recapture the memory of their last council meeting is that they have not yet met the expectations agreed upon at this meeting.

Since the spirit world always exists in now time, clients who hypnotically reenter this realm may judge themselves on their current life and thus become resistant to another council visitation. This is not common. Fortunately, I find that of those clients who are somewhat resistant about visiting their council, few remain so for very long. The attraction to the council is potent; many clients are so caught up with the positive aspects of what they always receive at council meetings that they refuse to go anywhere until they have had their chance for a council review.

Apparently, all souls visit members of their council at least once between lives and this usually happens not too long after their return from an incarnation. By far, this first meeting has the greatest effect on a soul because it involves evaluations of their progress. However, be prepared for some clients to pay a second visit to the council just before or after body selection as they get ready for a new life.

There seems to be no particular pattern for a soul having one or two visits between their lives. The soul may have had an especially difficult time with a past life, but I suspect the magnitude of severity, or karmic complexity, of the next life plays a major part in the council's decision to have the soul come for a second visit. It is possible the soul has had a long history of making the same mistakes and thus additional reinforcing may be required by the soul's council just before rebirth. The level of the soul is also a consideration because younger souls naturally require more support from guides and their council.

Most clients have profound feelings for the members of their council. Often, I hear the term "Elder" used to describe a council member, but other common identifications are the Wise Ones, the Sacred Committee, the Planners, and so on. I always begin this series of council questions with:

1. By what name do you wish me to call these beings?

When a client tells me they are ready to go before this body, I will inquire:

2. Do you go with someone or by yourself?

A majority of clients respond that their guide will accompany them, especially the Level I and II souls. I now ask:

3. Please describe your travel route. I would like to know what you see and do along the way and what happens when you arrive.

The trip never seems to last long and clients have the feeling that their council is not too far away from the location of their cluster group. A review of chapter six, the Council of Elders, in Destiny of Souls will demonstrate my findings about typical council settings and how they usually appear to people in trance (see also figure 6, reproduced in this appendix).

Often clients will describe a domed structure, which I feel is symbolic of an earthly spiritual shrine, temple, or even a hall of justice. Nevertheless, in no way do people see this enclosure as a courtroom with judges. This is an important distinction since clients describe their visions of spiritual structures using symbolic comparisons to images familiar to them on Earth. In the minds of clients, the council chamber represents a holy place of reverence. I am not being overly dramatic when I say that people who are still incarnating believe that when they are in a council chamber, they are close to God (or the Source).

From a theoretical standpoint, I feel it is not a coincidence that most everyone sees a large, spherical room for the council meetings. This circular, unbroken shape utilizes a concentrated energy field of superior thought where no energy escapes. The contained, refined energy is projected outward from the Elders and surrounds the still-incarnating soul with encouragement and enlightenment. I suspect the ringed design of the place of life selection has similar properties of powerful energy containment, but for a different use involving directors who focus timeline images for souls.

The moment the soul enters the council chamber, their guide appears nearby, usually in back of them. On some occasions I have had advanced souls who have entered the enclosure alone. Their guide is already in the room. Souls consider a council member, or Elder, to be a step or two above a senior guide. Your client will feel in awe of these wise beings. Sometimes you may sense a little anxiety in the voice of your client during their trip to the chamber. There are those souls who are bubbling over with anticipation, while others approach the council with quiet, serene contemplation.

As the client enters the council chamber, I will ask this question:

4. How many beings do you see waiting for you?

It is common for clients to respond by giving me a number between three and ten. The average is five to seven. Occasionally, a client might say that they see more than ten Elders. This is rare. While a larger number of council Elders in attendance can mean a more advanced soul is coming before them, you should be cautious in accepting a number higher than ten.

Besides a simple visual mistake, a large council gathering could also indicate they are having some sort of dialogue with each other, perhaps about a prior soul, that does not relate to your client's case. While you must be careful not to invalidate client statements, I do find that repeating question four as the client draws closer may reveal that some Elders are leaving. If they all stay, some won't seem to be participating in the upcoming proceedings with your client.

When the client approaches closer to the space where they will be interviewed, I'll continue with my series of questions about the council. These inquiries are not necessarily listed in an order suitable for every client and inevitably there will be variations depending upon the circumstances of individual council meetings.

5. I would like you to describe to me just how you are feeling right now.

This all-inclusive question should be asked more than once if necessary and at any time during the proceedings.

6. Is your guide in the chamber? If so, where is this guide located in relation to you?

Most guides stand in back and slightly to the left or right of the soul. Sometimes with a more advanced client the guide is adjacent to the council or even on the council.

7. Where do you position yourself in relation to your council?

   Most souls appear to move to a place directly in front.
8. Are you going to stand or will you sit?

   Almost always, souls will stand in front of the Elders.
9. Let's check again on exactly how many beings are here waiting for you. Please count them from left to right.
10. Are they standing or sitting?
11. If they are sitting down, please describe any sort of furniture you see in front of them.

    The average client visualizes the Elders sitting at a long, curved, or rectangular table.
12. Is the council positioned slightly above you, on some sort of dais, or are they at eye level, directly in front of you?

More often than not, the Elders are at eye level. The reason I am engaged with small details at this point is that I want to get my client accustomed to observing and reporting everything that is going on in a step-by-step fashion. This is a warm up for a very significant meeting and my questions will become more rigorous.

13. Look closely, do you see any gender characteristics among the council members? Can you identify the number of beings who appear as male or female, or are they all androgynous?

Frankly, many clients see their council composed of elderly males, which is a cultural stereotype representing wisdom. The more advanced souls will report genderless council members. They may also appear as elongated, translucent light forms.

14. Describe to me how each member is dressed.

When council members appear as human forms, they generally have robes. I will question the meaning associated with the color of these garments. Sometimes they are all dressed in white (clarity of thought) or purple (wisdom), but they may be dressed in a variety of individual colors that could indicate a particular talent or specialty, such as green for an Elder who is a healer. The meaning of certain robe colors may also relate directly to a soul's character or even the lack of an individual trait that is important for the soul to acquire for continued development.

15. Do you have the sense that one Elder will serve as a chairperson, moderator, or director of these proceedings?

Everyone could be an equal participant, but typically one council member will direct the agenda. If the client tells me there is a director, I will ask, "Where is this being located in relation to the others?" Almost always the answer is, "In the center." If there is a director, one or two others may make comments but rarely does every panel member address the soul, unless the council has less than four members. Moreover, you will have some clients who see the director as displaying a light which is larger and brighter than the other council members. If this is the case, I would ask, "Does larger and brighter mean this Elder is more powerful than the rest?" You will be told something to the effect, "No, it's so I will pay more attention to this being and what he is saying to me."

16. Is anyone wearing any sort of ornament or emblem you can identify?

This question refers to the fact that many clients see one or more council members wearing medallions around their neck or rings with precious stones. The stone colors denote specific concepts relating to the soul. I refer you to Destiny of Souls, chapter six, where I discuss signs and symbols in the spirit world. If only one panel member is wearing a medallion or ornament, it is frequently the moderator.

17. I want you to describe the design on this medallion and give me the meaning of what you see.

Some clients will tell you they cannot make out any lines or designs on these emblems. I always explain to the client that council members are not wearing these ornaments out of vanity or to indicate some sort of authority to impress the soul. These symbols have meaning to the soul and are reminders of a soul's personal power, potential, and karmic goals.

Therefore, I will instruct my client to look closer and to begin by telling me if the medallion (typically depicted as round and metal) is gold, silver, or bronze and if it is the size of a plum, orange, or grapefruit, and then ask them once again to describe the design and its meaning.

Other peripheral questions that might be asked at this early phase are:

18. Does the number and makeup of your council change after each life?
19. Is there anything different about the surroundings here since your last visit?
20. Do you have the sense your council is going to be easy on you this time or do they appear rather severe?

This last query about the demeanor of the Elders is a leading question designed to encourage a strong counter-response. I have never seen any evidence of jarring or harsh treatment from the Elders. On occasion, a council member may initially appear to my client as very serious or intense in their questioning but they are not austere or dictatorial. Council members can be challenging but they are not argumentative or judgmental. It is my impression the council is guided by a desire to assist the soul in an atmosphere of love, compassion, and understanding. I hope that a counter-response from a protesting client over my asking question twenty about severity will produce more information than I might otherwise receive.

When I know the council meeting is ready to get underway, I ask this question:

21. What is the first thing you hear in your mind and which Elder addresses you?

Normally at this stage there will be a welcoming statement from the director or chairperson and then some sort of opening exchange will follow in a slow, gentle manner, as in the following:

Elder: So, you are with us again; welcome back.

Soul: I'm glad to be back.

Elder: Good, now tell us how you feel about your last life?

Soul: I think it was all right . . . but I guess I could have done much better.

Elder: In what way do you see that you could have done more for yourself and others?

In Journey of Souls there is a case quote that I always try to remember when I have clients before their council:

> The Elders are all-knowing about my entire span of lives but they are not as directive as one might think. They want my input to assess my motivations and strength of resolve.

Another case example indicating the way in which council evaluations are conducted is as follows:

> When the Elders begin to talk to me there is an initial greeting and I am asked to express my thoughts about my progress. My guide is mentally helping me but he does not interfere. My participation in the events of my last life are reviewed and compared to my actions with similar events in my other lives. The Elders seem to be evaluating how my host bodies worked to benefit or hinder me and maybe they are considering the type of body appropriate to my next test. I am questioned about my motivation and goals and if I am happy. There is a give and take between us because nothing can be hidden from them. The council is aware of all my good and bad character traits. They are encouraging and telling me not to be too hard on myself.

Besides the multitude of questions you will want to ask during soul-Elder exchanges, I will list some of my own you might consider:

22. Is there a reason why a particular Elder is on your panel?
23. Does one panel member have a certain area of expertise or special interest when they question you that relates directly to your own interests and experience?
24. What do the Elders say about your progress that was not discussed with your guide in orientation or at any other time?
25. During these proceedings, does your guide have any input about your progress?
26. What is your opinion about the Elders' general attitude toward the way you lived your last life?
27. Do the council members make any comments about your current state of advancement compared to all your former lives?
28. In terms of evaluation, does anyone on the council offer constructive criticism or specific encouragement toward you?
29. Are the statements given to you by this council any different from other council meetings you have attended after former lives?
30. What are your overall feelings about yourself as the council meeting draws to a close?
31. Is there anything else you wish to say to your director or chairperson before we leave the council chamber? What message is being given to you that could be useful in your current life?

I never end a council meeting without asking question thirty-one because so much can be learned about your client's life today in the timeless spiritual atmosphere of this visualization.

On the return trip back to their cluster I often have interesting exchanges with my clients. It is a time of processing and they are in a reflective mood. It is strange but quite often guides do not accompany the soul back to their clusters. My subjects don't seem to know why but I suspect their guides may be engaged with matters relating to the just-completed meeting. Sometimes on these return trips I will ask a client, "Do any other members of your group go before the same council?" Typically, soul companions go before different councils. This probably has to do with the differences between soul character, talent, and motivations, especially at the lower levels of advancement. Another point I should mention is that souls do not appear to discuss these proceedings later with their friends. It is considered too private a matter for public discussion as well as a violation of trust between the soul and their council.

41

Therapeutic Opportunities during Council Visitations

While your client is in the council meeting room, you might ask the question:
>Do you think there is a higher being in this room at a greater level than the Elders?

I have had clients describe a "Presence" whom they consider a superior, Godlike source that monitors the council itself. Those clients who do have this acute awareness are profoundly moved. I give case examples of reports about the Presence in chapter six of Destiny of Souls.

When your client is undergoing interviews by the wise beings who probably placed them on Earth, it is one of the most meaningful aspects of the entire session. The psychological benefits are enormous. This is because the client is both an observer using the mind of their current body, as well as a participant utilizing their immortal soul-mind. You will find similar (but not with quite the same impact) insightful opportunities exist later in the space of life selection, when your client chooses their body.

The overall individual guidance offered by our guides is vital to a soul's well-being. Yet I believe the interviews of a single council meeting greatly exceed that of orientation debriefings after a life because council meetings are so far-reaching in terms of spiritual planning and management. When the Elders are reviewing the progress of the souls who come before them, their keen evaluations encompass the soul's entire existence. You are able to look at highlights of many past life scripts through the interactions between a client and council members. As old memories resurface, your client's perceptions about who they really are as an immortal being will be of great consequence in the process of self-discovery.

In my view, there is a privacy of the mind that is released from a superconscious soul-state which transcends other forms of therapy. While in a deep trance state in front of our council the conscious mind is much less inhibited by disclosure. This is because the soul- mind is interacting with the human brain to provide basic truths about one's real self. Clients are less afraid to admit the secrets they know to be true about their character when reporting to you about their experiences before a group of wise, benevolent advisors.

However, having said all this, I want to make it clear that your client will not be able to recall intimate details of their council meeting. I suspect some of this blockage of total recall is by design because the client is not spiritually ready in their current life to receive it. Other aspects of a council meeting may not be revealed because the client is not psychologically prepared. The LBL therapist should seek to determine if client resistance to recall during a council meeting is Elder-directed or is information being withheld from a desire by the client to avoid painful analyzation of mistakes and shortcomings.

Be aware that both Elders and guides are apparently able to screen the thoughts they transmit to the returning soul as well. This will reduce your client's ability to reconstruct a complete picture of what is going on at all times during the council meeting. I have had only a very few highly advanced clients who were able to pick up any conversation between council members that were not expressly directed to the soul. Here is an unusual example:

Dr. N: While you are communicating with the director of your council, what do you think is transpiring between the other members?

Subject: They communicate with each other to compare examples of other cases like mine.

Dr. N: Please explain this further.

Subject: I can't read much, but they seem to be comparing methods which have worked with other souls to determine what might be the best approach for me in my next body.

Dr. N: As you listen, do you find this information helpful to you in any way?

Subject: Not really. The communication is too abstract and rapid and I only can catch fragments between the mental barriers. Besides, I must keep my attention focused on the director.

In the spirit world, the power of soul blocking with telepathic communications and conversely the ability to read through the blocks of others seem to increase with soul advancement. Certainly, the Elders do block most of their communication between themselves from souls who appear before them. To me, this seems a bit unfair to the still-incarnating soul, but my clients feel comforted that what they are supposed to know will eventually be revealed to them.

It is not easy for the spiritual regressionist to determine if certain details are being blocked by the client or the Elders themselves. Selective amnesia exists within each client. I have come to believe that what a client is supposed to know at this juncture in their life will be uncovered during the session. The rest must come from within each client, to be released later in life at the proper time.

While I believe it is the task of LBL therapists to work as hard as they can to extract information when clients are in the presence of teachers, there are boundaries. Once in a great while

I hear of an inexperienced or unprofessional hypnotherapist who will try to evoke responses from a unsuspecting subject by improperly encouraging transference and engaging in projection and countertransference. During hypnosis, when the subject experiences a temporary displacement of feelings onto the therapist, this is transference. There are susceptible clients, especially those with unresolved emotional attitudes connected with early bonding experiences in childhood, who wish to please the therapist and essentially make them a parent. Thus transference becomes a dependency issue.

For instance, a client may project the following: "I see you (the facilitator) in my spirit group!" Since the odds against this are astronomical, my suggestion is to always assume such a statement is an initial knee-jerk reaction relating to their warm feelings about you. As an LBL professional, you represent a trusted spiritual advisor who is engaged in connecting people to their spiritual history. My advice is to gently remind your client that finding you in their spirit group is highly doubtful considering there must be billions of soul groups involving people on Earth. Thank them for the compliment and explain that you have heard this before from others and it would be a good idea to take a closer look at each member of their soul group. It is best to remove this misinterpretation as rapidly as possible.

Countertransference results when an inept therapist feeds into this dependency need by encouraging their subject's transference and by projecting themselves into client visualizations. My worst example of this sort of practice in LBL work would be, "Do you see me on your council?" Another is, "Do you see me as one of your spirit guides?" Perhaps a facilitator with a poor ego structure feels dissatisfied with what the client is producing, or they may want to project their own wishes onto the subject, or feel in some misguided way that they are nurturing.

In any case, this clumsy approach not only displays professional ignorance but is unethical and a violation of trust. Fortunately, these circumstances are rare and the large majority of subjects are both cognitive and too independent of spirit to allow a facilitator to project themselves into scenes. Spiritual regression connects both parties at various energy levels and therefore when transference problems arise they inhibit a free, unbiased flow of information unless shut down immediately.

Nevertheless, there is no reason why an LBL therapist should be inhibited entirely from personalizing questions to advance the spiritual regression session. About the time when a council meeting is getting underway, I might ask:

> Why do you feel at this point in your life these wise teachers have mentally encouraged you to seek out my assistance in helping you access information about your soul life?

This inquiry invites thoughts of synchronicity—that is, events that come together at a certain time for a reason. Most clients pause before they answer this question and I will not speak again until they do. I have mentioned that subjects in hypnosis respond slowly to probing questions because they are receiving more thoughts and experiencing greater imagery than what they are reporting to you. It is best to be very patient. It is true that you could ask the conscious client during intake what they specifically want to know from their council about their current life. However, I feel the broader issue of why a client is seeking spiritual guidance through your facilitation at this time in their life will have more relevance if this question is addressed in front of the Elders.

Of course every client has ongoing core issues but many are at a crossroad when they come to see you. Are they going to continue with the same pattern of living or are they ready to make positive mental changes? In my own practice I often hear the remark, "I thought I really needed to see you last year during a crisis but now is a better time because I am calmer and more reflective." Clients do feel a sense of purpose about their session. This becomes evident during council meetings with both Elders and guides present because they are a soul's primary guardians. I should also add that many clients have observed that my own guide was in the office assisting me from behind my chair. There have been times when I felt this as well.

With regard to addressing issues in a client's current life, one should understand that in the spirit world souls exist in now time, which is not limited by timelines and therefore is not absolute. This will be especially helpful to you during council meetings. I remind my subjects that the beauty of now time in the spirit world is that I am able to move them forward, backward, or suspend the council proceedings temporarily. This is an excellent therapeutic tool during spiritual regression.

For example, in the middle of a council meeting we may be having a discussion about making choices in life. I can freeze the action and place the meeting on hold while taking my client to the place of life selection to discuss choices that were made about their current body, and then return them to the council. This gives the meeting more depth. You may also wish to suspend the council to transport your client to some significant event in their current life or any other life that has direct relevance to a specific topic under discussion.

Since council meetings take place after a past life, the events that have brought an inquiring client to you have technically not yet happened in current linear time. This does not limit current life therapy. Because the spirit world exists in a timeless domain where all possible nows abide together, the sequence of physical and biological events from one former body to a new current body poses no restrictions for analysis. I often say:

> Look carefully at your council right now and tell me how they feel you are doing at this time in your current life.

With the subject's soul fully exposed to the scrutiny of the Elders, this question presents an opportunity for the spiritual regressionist to uncover the deeper issues surrounding self-concept. At this juncture it is fitting that we try to clarify misperceptions, assist clients in identifying what is unique about them, help them come to a greater understanding about patterns of behavior, and foster an awareness to make optimal use of their strengths and weaknesses.

I feel clients in a superconscious trance state are better able to interpret their own internal behavior through increased insight. I know that I am only an intermediary for more powerful spiritual forces in my client's existence. People ask, "If time in the spirit world is not an absolute, can we see into the future as well as the past in a superconscious state?" It is possible to a small degree with a few clients but progression, in my view, is unreliable. The reason seeing into the future from a current life is generally not possible goes to issues of self-discovery, free will, and nondeterministic paths of choice. I will have more to say about future time progression under Life and Body Selection later in Part Five.

Before closing these sections on council meetings, I should add that even though you decide to take your client to the place of life selection in the middle of a council meeting, this does not preclude you from doing so again in more detail later as the session draws to a close. In many cases you will find it meaningful for the client to return once more to the place of life selection for more thorough discussions about their current body choice. As I have said before, subjects in LBL regression do not necessarily visualize an orderly progression through the spirit world, consisting of going to orientations, encountering friends, and meeting members of their council. Having the flexibility and creativity to move your subject back and forth in different spatial areas at appropriate moments in the session will serve you well.

42

Reviewing Past Life Incarnations

With many LBL cases, the best time to discuss a client's former incarnations is either during a council meeting or right afterward. However, what if your client finds themselves in a library, a classroom, or a space of solitude? Places of this nature are equally suitable to discuss past life highlights. Reviewing certain aspects of significant past lives in your client's history, in conjunction with their greater understanding of soul character, is therapeutically important. The client is brought to a greater awareness of their identity and the fact that they are a unique being. The immortal character of souls is shaped by the direction of will, desire, and imagination, while being influenced in actions and deeds from many bodies. I want to know about the effects and end result from this past life behavior.

Human society, especially in areas of high population, can cause one to feel isolated, empty, and unable to commit if we are not sure who we are in the scheme of things. A vital component to reviewing past lives is uncovering a client's true identity by analyzing a variety of bodies. I have a series of questions for the client in this regard:

1. How much is your soul-ego influenced by the brain of each body you choose? Do some bodies make it more difficult than others to maintain your permanent identity?
2. What is your most important individual characteristic as a soul that defines the real you that would be carried from life to life?

3. Do you choose to be one gender more than another in your lives?
4. Are you attracted to being in bodies in certain parts of the world for cultural and geographic reasons?
5. What sort of life are you most comfortable living?
6. Of all your past lives, tell me what life was the most significant and productive.

By bringing in your client's personal identification with former bodies it is easier to understand why certain choices were made in other lifetimes that might relate to their current life. I look for the expression of satisfaction when a particular effect is achieved—or disappointment when it is not achieved—in these lifetimes. You may find that those clients who come to you with past life regression experience probably have not been asked relevant questions about their soul identity in all these different bodies. An LBL session will add dimension to these earlier past life sessions.

In condensing past life reviews with a full LBL regression, I might touch on a couple of significant lives with an overview approach. In this context, there is one question I always ask of everyone:

8. When was your first life on Earth?

Having some familiarity with the history of world civilizations and their rise and fall is invaluable. Your client might respond to the "first life" question by describing membership in a Stone Age tribe some 50,000 to 100,000 years ago in the Paleolithic era. Another client will see themselves in a Neolithic period perhaps 5,000 to 10,000 years ago. Many clients remember their first life as being in the early civilizations of Egypt and Mesopotamia perhaps 3,000 to 5,000 years ago. Unless you have a very young soul with few past lives, your client will probably not be able to remember most of their past lives except those where they experienced their greatest accomplishments. Even so, most people can recall their first life on Earth.

What about visitations to Earth by the souls of your clients who were in alien bodies? While you will have hybrid souls whose early physical incarnations were on other planets before coming to Earth, it is very rare to have a client who actually visited Earth in an alien body. They may have been engaged in some sort of colonization attempt early in our cultural history or just made a brief visit. Out of all my cases I have had only a handful of such people. I wrote an article about these anomalies in my practice for Fate magazine in the March 2001 issue.

When you ask the question, "Where are you during your first life on Earth?" be prepared for some clients to declare, "I'm in Atlantis." I have discussed the Atlantis Attraction Syndrome earlier in Part Three under Checking Conscious Interference, relating to preconceived bias. This "lost eighth continent" was thought to exist around 10,000 years ago. I am curious about this legend myself but I am also skeptical. While I must acknowledge an Atlantis could have existed on Earth in some form, it still falls under the heading of unproven mythology.

Without negating initial reactions from some clients about having a life in Atlantis, I want LBL therapists to know that it is quite possible you are dealing with a hybrid soul in these situations. I have many references to hybrids listed in Destiny of Souls. Clients who have the feeling their first lives were in Atlantis may actually be hybrid souls who had thousands of years of prior incarnations on a physical world resembling the geographic legend of Atlantis. These lives ended for the soul before they began coming to Earth. I have not found that we have intermittent lives on other planets between our Earth lives.

When working with a hybrid soul, you could face psychological challenges. These people may not have made healthy adjustments to life on Earth. Their association with a human brain and the heavy energy density of the human body could still be daunting. I have had clients who feel their Earth body is alien. The incidence of suicide among hybrids in their first lives on Earth is higher than non-hybrids. If you do have a hybrid soul as a client, there are certain basic questions you will want to ask about their experiences on an alien world:

1. Can you tell me if this planet is part of our universe or in another dimension?
2. If it is in our universe, could this planet be in our own Milky Way galaxy and perhaps near Earth?
3. Does it still exist and what is its name?
4. Is it a physical or a mental world?
   a. (If a mental world) Describe this world and your place in it.
   b. (If a physical world) Would you say this world was larger or smaller than the size of Earth?
5. Please compare the topography of this world to Earth in terms of mountains, deserts, oceans, and atmosphere.
6. If this planet had organic life, what was the most intelligent form? (Usually this form was the client's body while incarnating.)
7. Tell me what you looked like on this planet, what were your thoughts, and what were your range of activities.
8. Why did you stop incarnating on this world and decide to come to Earth?
9. Explain the differences in mental makeup between your body on this alien world and your human body on Earth.
10. Compare the technology of this world to Earth.
11. Is there anyone in your lives on Earth who was with you on this world?

In your review of past lives, sometimes you will wonder about the possibility of outside influences on those clients who claim that all their incarnations were on Earth. Here are two case quotes as examples:

A. In my early lives on Earth I wanted to cause a shift of consciousness from this primitive brain to make it more human.

B. One of my significant early lives was just before the last Ice Age (25,000 years ago) where I raised the consciousness of my tribe by discovering an herb mixed with a mineral which calmed the nervous system and sharpened perceptions of the brain. This made my people less primitive and more rational.

In summary, keep in mind that all past life experiences affect soul development, some more than others. However, it is while a subject is visualizing life in the spirit world that we can help them correlate the lessons from these experiences into their life today. The choice of each body in each lifetime is actually the psychological sum of all previous body choices both here and on other planets.

At the beginning of Part Four in this text, I discussed the occasional need to desensitize trauma from past life death scenes before regressing clients into the spirit world. There is no question former negative body imprints can affect the lives of some people today. Having said that, I believe this area of past life therapy has been dramatically overblown while the healing properties of life between lives has not been given due consideration. This is because LBL therapy is a new field.

There are highly qualified past life therapists who have strong opinions about the effects of psychological damage to a soul from former lives that has been transmitted into a current body. They place heavy emphasis on current mental distress involving fear and anger originating from being a victim in some lives and guilt over being a perpetrator of wrongdoing in others. They take this idea further with a belief that residuals of negative karmic patterns still exist, even though the lessons have been learned, and therefore must be expunged. This is an old concept that requires reexamination. Tibetan mysticism and Eastern religious philosophy declare that our consciousness is influenced by what is called "dependent origination." Samskaras is a term the ancients used to describe negative karmic patterns that pass from body to body and plague one's psyche. These doctrines have influenced past life therapy.

I would argue that the ancients did not possess the cognitive knowledge we have today about the spirit world. Many past life practitioners not familiar with LBL therapy fail to take into consideration that negative thoughts and feelings from our past lives are largely healed between lives in the spirit world. It is easy to blame the problems that trouble us on negative past life imprints. Frankly, even during the busiest years of my practice I found only a low percentage of clients were seriously affected by past life body imprints. If this is true, then why are souls so often conflicted? I feel the answer lies in the fact that for many people mental distress is the result of a difficult soul-body connection. I will review this aspect of LBL therapy in more detail in my section on Connections Between the Body and Soul later in Part Five.

43

Surveying Other Spirit World Activities

At some point after your client's council visit and before their transition to the space of life selection, I suggest asking a catch-all question:

> Would you provide me with details of your other activities in the spirit world? I am thinking of those periods when you are not being evaluated by counselors or undergoing specific training. Perhaps we could start with your most favorite recreational activity.

In chapter seven in Destiny of Souls under recreational activities, there are many sections dealing with a variety of soul activities you might wish to review from time to time for ideas. Of course, what one client considers recreation another might feel is a training activity. The following is a list of spiritual activity categories that could prove fruitful in your investigations:

A. Areas inside the spirit world where souls are trained to use their energy creatively.
B. Areas outside the spirit world, which could include uninhabited physical worlds where souls can practice their skills in manipulating energy to create both animate and inanimate objects.
C. Areas in other dimensions, including mental worlds, where souls travel to study or play.

D. Areas that are communal where souls may go for pure recreation involving singing, dancing, telling stories, and playing games.
E. Areas of solitude for study and reflection.
F. Areas of assembly where souls gather with others in activities such as listening to lectures by roving teachers.

There are many varieties of inquiry within these general categories. An example would be expanding category C, about interdimensional travel, with these questions:

> Why are you an interdimensional traveler?
>
> Is our reality combined within the same dimensional space as another reality?
>
> How many dimensions are you able to visit and what is the difference between them and our universe?
>
> Do you see and interact with other intelligent beings in these interdimensional realities?
>
> Are you involved with both physical and mental dimensions? If so, describe the differences.

Assisting a client in the examination of a full range of activities will reveal many aspects of their character and level of advancement. Clients whose souls are solidly in Level III and above are probably specializing in some activity which suits their talents, interests, and experience. I have outlined some of these specialty areas in chapter eight under the advancing soul in Destiny of Souls.

Reviewing your client's spirit world activities also enables you to check the levels of collective progress with their spiritual companions. In this context, I would draw your attention to an activity I call spiritual psychodrama between soul companions that can produce a mine of information.

I suppose psychodrama could come under the category of classroom activities but I often see this work conducted away from classroom settings and teachers. It has the appearance of a study group with the evaluation of performance conducted by peers. You will have clients who do not engage in psychodrama in soul groups, but the ones that do find it very instructive in comparing their behavior in a physical body with friends. I think this activity is worthy of particular attention in LBL therapy. You might begin your inquiry with this question:

> Do you engage in any activity in the spirit world with your friends where you evaluate each other's performance from the previous life?

There are soul groups who engage in the practice of role-playing where they re-create their physical lives, with each soul companion assuming different roles. It is rather like a room full of people playing duplicate bridge. This is done to see who can employ the best strategy for the most productive life. One soul companion will challenge another to switch roles in the same body as a means of comparison, with "the judges" being their friends. While psychodrama is looked upon as a game, with a lot of teasing and fun, it is also instructive.

The whole exercise is designed for souls to better understand how certain bodies and minds are selected for particular tasks in a given set of circumstances. The re-creation of interactive scenes allows you to sit in while your client and their soul companions study all the major variables in any given former life situation. Naturally, a number of former predicaments involving problem solving relate to current client issues. There are many conclusions you could draw from listening to a scene involving psychodrama. Here are three examples:

1. Did your client act as a lone wolf or function in collaboration with others when there was a difficult choice to be made at a crossroad in life?
2. Was this choice motivated by self-interest or predicated by a desire to bring positive change into the situation, especially if it involved the lives of others?

3. In what ways has your client's responses to difficult situations, especially those involving relationships, changed in their current life as a result of new perceptions gained from psychodrama after former lives?

You will find that many of the actors in this spirit world play are on-stage again with meaningful roles in your client's current life drama.

When searching for clues relating to particular issues in your client's life, it is wise to pay attention to all aspects of their spirit world activities. Every client has a different twist to their spiritual memories. A line of inquiry could work well for one client but not for another. You will have clients who have only hazy memories about their spiritual life away from guides and Elders, while others will give graphic details about many things, providing you ask. Never forget that the average client does not automatically volunteer information. In any session it is easy to miss a signpost if you are not methodical in your questioning. I will give a case illustration of a near oversight on my part involving spiritual activities.

I was about ready to bring Jack's LBL session to a close when I asked him, as an afterthought, "Was there any sort of instruction we missed between your last life and current life that you are supposed to be working on today?" After a long pause, Jack said, "Oh, I guess you must mean that time when I sat in on a visiting lecturer's class with fifteen other souls I didn't know." I had no idea what Jack was talking about but I replied in my most confident manner, "Yes, that class. On the count of three, I want you to return to this class and tell me all about it . . . one, two, three!"

Jack then told me he was asked to attend a "what if" class conducted in an assembly area that looked like a small Greco-Roman temple with circular seats. An instructor was in the center. The "what if" drill consisted of the instructor asking each soul in attendance what they would do in a particular circumstance during an incarnation. When Jack's turn came I really did not know what to expect. His face grew dark and he spoke in a halting voice:

> Oh . . . that's it! Mine . . . was about kindness to animals . . . and I'm falling down. In my past lives, I had been either cruel or indifferent to animals, particularly with the horses I rode in battle. (after a long pause) I dislike cats . . . I am not very kind to my dog . . . they are here to teach me compassion. I've got to remember this! The teacher is giving me my "what if" question and it's about the treatment of pets.

Perhaps at first glance my client's vision of this activity may not seem of great consequence in the scheme of other karmic issues. This would be a wrong assumption. Jack and I were able to explore his attitude toward the broader issues of kindness and compassion in his life and how the attributes of animals are capable of enriching our understanding of all living things. Jack does not like pets but his family insists on having them.

On questioning Jack further as to why this spiritual lecturer singled him out for a "what if" question involving his treatment of animals in former lives, we discovered it was about prejudice toward what he considered "a lower form of life." Since animals are different from us they are undervalued and taken for granted by some people. Probing further, we discovered that animals were the outward manifestation of Jack's need to feel superior to people who were different from himself. This particular spiritual activity was a wake-up call before his current life. It was fortunate that we were able to uncover Jack's memory about this event before the end of the session.

As you complete your line of questioning about the many spiritual activities of your clients, be aware of the differences in perception between the more advanced souls and everyone else. Perhaps the limitations of our physical brain impose a filter for soul information from the spirit world. The average client tends to separate out one visual image or activity at a time in their reporting. A few clients, however, find a constant unification of spiritual wisdom. They appear to receive a simultaneous flow of significant messages from all their soul activities.

44

Life and Body Selection

The last major phase of a spiritual regression session is conveying your client back to the region where they viewed their current body just before incarnation. Souls don't go to this spatial area unless they are ready to incarnate into another life. Chapters twelve and thirteen in Journey of Souls and chapter nine in Destiny of Souls give many details about how clients view their next life and the bodies offered to them for this new life. As with other spatial areas in the spirit world having specific functions, your clients will give you different names for this zone. The most common are the Place of Life Selection, the Screening Room, or the Ring of Destiny.

You will find that the space of life selection and body review is usually visualized as round with large panels or screens that appear as transparent sheets of liquid energy. It is presented as a theater-in-the-round where futuristic scenes of people and events are displayed for the soul who is ready to enter a new life. The actions of your clients in this space will fall into two categories:

A. Souls who prefer to just observe the scenes.
B. Souls who wish to actually participate by entering the scenes of their choosing.

These two preferences in the life selection room depend on the character of the soul, their particular inclinations at the time of the visit, and the nature of the life to come. Some souls are just accepting, especially the younger ones, while others have more of an analytical and investigative nature.

From the panels in front of them, many souls seem to be able to control the movement of scenes that show a number of possible futures in various lives. It seems logical that manipulations are performed by the soul-mind, yet clients report using earthly mechanical descriptions to describe this function with such terms as buttons, knobs, dials, and levers. In my books, I have said that for the most part the specialists or directors who control this space are not seen by the soul. Yet the incarnating soul is aware someone is in charge, monitoring the action. Some souls have their guide with them, while others do not.

My cases indicate that the timelines involved with events and chronological periods associated with different bodies shown in the panels are edited. This depends on the nature of the upcoming life, the karmic lessons to be addressed, and the soul involved. Among the many variables here is the fact that the same soul may be given more viewing options for some lives and less in others, just as we are given more body choices before some lives than others. You will have clients who see most of the life to come in increments of childhood, adolescence, adulthood, and old age while another individual might see only one short segment of their life.

Prior to some lives, your client will be offered only one or two body choices. At other visits to the place of life selection they may be given up to five. There is always a leading candidate. Souls seem to know which body would be their best choice for learning and they usually choose it. For instance, your client might say there are three options: an easy, moderately accommodating, or very difficult body. Also, the life choices for those bodies could be defined as uncomplicated, rather hard, or arduous. The reasons for this range of choices involving the next life depend upon motivational desires and certain karmic issues as well as the evolutionary age and past performance of the soul. Quite often your client will be unable to explain the rationale and wisdom behind all the variables connected with a particular life and the body offerings for that life.

Future timelines are an integral part of the life selection screening rooms. In physical Earth time, the screens seem to be offering snapshots of events with possibilities and probabilities. Apparently, there is no certainty of any event in future time on Earth because then our lives would be totally deterministic, with no free will. The laboratory of Earth would be a poor testing school if we were governed by fate. I believe there are an indefinite number of futures connected to a present in the now time of the spirit world. And yet, while there must be many futures, souls seem to view the most likely futures in a matrix of possibilities and probabilities. On the screens, events and opportunities of a future life may be enlarged and drawn out or reduced in size for soul analysis. It is like looking at the large trunks and smaller branches of trees. I use this analogy because some timelines combined with certain life scenes seem more prominent than others.

I have already spoken about how now time in the spirit world seems to be a conglomeration of past, present, and future. Picture streams of energy waves containing events flowing out into the future and back from the past meeting in the center, at the vortex of the spirit world. Souls from Earth are able to visualize sitting in the library and watching a computer-like screen displaying all the nuances of their past lives. In the life selection room they are given the same opportunities for examination of the immediate future but in less overall detail. Since we are given samples of the future, this engagement must come under the heading of future time progression.

My feelings on timelines and free will are expressed more fully in chapter nine of Destiny of Souls. I will just add here that there are those Quantum Theory scientists who believe that we will always find ourselves in now events that have high probabilities and so this would tip the scales toward determinism. Thus, because of fewer possibilities, the future would make free will less equal due to predeterminism. However, my clients are convinced that the future offers many different choices, and each now frame of time exists simultaneously with all the other possible nows. We cannot know if alternating realities are interlocking within one reality or parallel realities exist adjacent to one another.

It is quite possible that in the now time of the spirit world, events on Earth are not actually moving but may only be on different timelines that seem to move in our aging physical universe. What I believe is that with every situational event people have the opportunity to make choices and effect mid-course corrections in their lives. Because we can approach the same event in different ways, the outcome of these events that affect us can be altered. I ask those who think events cannot be changed by free will if they can at least accept the fact that our reaction and behavior toward those events can make some difference to the outcome.

Some potential clients are curious if I conduct hypnosis progression. I do not. In the life selection room, apparently souls are only able to view scenes in their next life and not beyond. Incidentally, if I have a forty-year-old client reviewing what he saw before his current life, this person is not going to be able to relate anything beyond the age of forty. Events beyond forty have not yet happened so he can't peek!

Experimenting earlier in my career with future time progression, I found most people are blocked by their guides from seeing lives far into the future. This allows for long-term self-discovery by the soul. Once in a while a client will get a flash of a possible future, such as being on a starship in the twenty-third century, but these brief pictures are hazy and indistinct. In my "Star Trek" cases I couldn't help but feel that their conscious desires (such as wanting to be a starship commander) interfered with objective reporting and became wishful thinking. Most clients believe trying to look into the future is something that is best left to the planners. The bottom line for me is that I do not think attempts to facilitate future time hypnosis progression is productive in LBL therapy.

Once you have prepared your client for the life selection room, you will be a witness to the decision-making involved with their current life and body. The following series of questions will hopefully elicit meaningful information:

1. How are you notified it is time to reincarnate and who tells you?
2. Would you describe your desire to come forward again as strong, moderate, slight, or resistant?
3. Have you ever said you were not ready for a new life? If so, what were the circumstances and final results?
4. Do you go to the place of life selection alone or with your guide?
5. Are you aware of any other higher beings working in the life selection room?
6. Describe the surroundings and tell me what you see and do.
7. How many body choices are available to you? Please describe each in detail.
8. What do you think each body offers you?
9. Is there a leading body candidate and was this the body you chose? Why did you reject the others?
10. When you see the body you chose in your current life, do you see it on the screens in live action? Can you regulate the action yourself, or does it seem someone else is controlling the movement of scenes for you?
11. Are you an observer or do you actually enter scenes of your current life as a participant?
12. What scene interests you the most and why?
13. What did you learn before you came to the place of life selection that helped you make the decision for a certain body?

14. While you are watching a variety of life scenes, are some more appropriate for certain body choices than others?
15. What does this body mean to you in terms of advantages and disadvantages? Explain the most significant positive and negative aspects of your body.
16. How does the brain of this body differ from other recent bodies you have occupied?
17. What is your primary mission in life and has it changed from what you see now in the life selection room?
18. Are the goals in this life different from other lives? If so, in what way?
19. Do you see certain people on the screens you are supposed to work with in this life?
20. Is there anything you see on the screens that we have not discussed? Is some entity preventing you from telling me everything you see?

There are many ways in which clients describe this spiritual experience. Some will give you running descriptions of all the scenes, while others are rather vague. You will have clients who will watch or participate in the scenes for a while and then don't want to see any more of their future life once they make their body choice. There are souls who have the attitude, "I trust they know what they are doing and I don't need to see anything." Always keep in mind that while your client is visualizing their experience in the life selection room they are capable of answering questions about their current life. The most obvious inquiry near the end of the life selection experience would be a follow-up to question sixteen:

> Are you living your life according to what you are viewing on the screens? If not, what is different and why?

45

Connections between Body and Soul

In the life selection room, some clients first see the body they will eventually occupy without their soul. This is because the live action has not yet begun onscreen. I remember a client telling me, "Initially we look at images of bodies lined up for us with no souls. They have their brains but are robotic, empty things." Once the screens are activated, your clients will rapidly connect with these bodies so they can see and feel what it would be like for their soul to be part of that body.

Once in a while a client will tell you they are rejecting a body because "it doesn't feel right." On very rare occasions you could have a client say they made a mistake in their body choice in a former life and asked to be released from that body during the first month after their entry into the fetus. Another soul will take this assignment. However, out of all my cases, not once have I ever had a walk-in soul who joined a body after birth. I try not to be preachy in my LBL training classes but there are hypnosis practitioners who are attracted to the walk-in theory and this does bother me.

My views on this subject are expressed in chapter three of *Destiny of Souls*. I know anything is possible but my clients deny walk-ins exist because our spiritual masters are too wise to allow for such an abomination as possession of the mind by other entities. The whole concept about outside entities who are able to occupy our minds is based on superstition and fear from the

Middle Ages. People who disagree with me argue that the walk-in is supposed to be engaged in an act of benevolence.

If you read my prior case studies on how souls join the fetus to meld with the developing human brain, you will see it is a slow, delicate process of incredible subtlety. A good example is Nancy's case that I describe in this text on page 51. The probing by the soul begins gently, carefully following the neurotransmitters of the brain while matching their own energy vibrations with the mind of the baby. Just imagine the shock to the adult human mind for one soul to substitute the energy of its immortal character for another in mid-life. I believe this would lead to either insanity or death.

Integration of a soul with the human brain is one of the most complex elements of spiritual regression. I discuss the many aspects of the soul-brain partnership through case studies in both my books. Essentially, most people feel reasonably comfortable with the duality of soul and brain that exists within their bodies. Still, there are others who may be moderately or even severely disturbed by the relationship. The LBL therapist must be cautious about making judgements with regard to the source of a client's mental disturbances.

For instance, people have often asked me if the underlying cause of Multiple Personality Disorder (MPD) could be a reoccurrence of personalities surfacing from former lives. I believe MPD represents massive repression of a single current personality traumatized by earlier events in this lifetime. The mentally ill MPD wishes to dissociate themselves from painful memories, often connected with childhood abuse. They escape into other non-past life personalities to avoid the reality of their own psyche. With the ordinary person, I believe a disruptive association between the soul and brain (soul duality) is much more likely than any MPD symptoms to create confusion about who we really are.

Another consideration about mental illness is the fact that certain bodies have a predisposition to abnormal brain chemistry and hormonal imbalances. Combine this with physical and emotional abuse as a child and you have a formula for a disturbed mind. I feel that if such a mind has a younger, inexperienced soul they are less able to cope and thus become contaminated and even trapped inside a sick biological mind. Thus the soul is unable to function properly.

The soul has an immortal character that is combined with a human brain and central nervous system, producing a given emotional temperament in our bodies. This melding creates one temporary personality in one lifetime. I call this essence the Principle of Self. Personal identity involves both conscious and unconscious memories and thus finding our real self can be elusive. In forming a perception of who we really are, people rely too much on examining their emotional and sensory reactions to information from the brain. The physical mind can fool us into believing we are who we might think we are based upon environmental influences from this planet and our emotional reaction to them.

Self is broadly identified by thoughts, memories, and perceptions of life that are influenced by an immortal consciousness, our soul. We look in the mirror and ask, "Why am I me?" Adding to this confusion over identity, our personality (our soul-ego and biological ego) develops and changes in uneven ways throughout a lifetime. While the biological ego changes rapidly over one life, the evolution of the soul's ego takes much longer. The core self provides the underpinning of our real personhood that influences emotional temperament and personality. All these elements are integrated into one human being. I believe that when this delicate integration is fractured, it fosters mental illness and perhaps criminal behavior.

When our soul-self is reached, we are able to perceive the internal distinctions of our immortal character. This gives us a deep sense of true individuality and a better conceptual understanding of who we really are as a whole person. Thus, LBL therapy seeks to help the client recognize their complete self by recovering unconscious memories of the joining of mind and body. LBL therapy is actually a spiritual quest for better self-understanding.

A client's soul-self may be quite different or rather similar to the emotional temperament of their host body. Souls rely on spirit-world planners to find the best candidates for a partnership that will address their strengths and weaknesses. The choice of a particular body is intended to combine a soul's character defects and strengths with certain strong and weak human emotional temperaments to produce specific trait combinations for mutual benefit. The biological mind of a human being is linked to a soul who then provides imagination, intuition, insight, and conscience. With this union we are one person dealing with two internal ego forces inside us during life. This combination represents the duality of mind and spirit in our bodies.

The two egos may blend well or show conflicting impulses leading to manifestations of neurotic anxiety. They may be in opposition or in conjunction with one another. Just because you find the two egos in opposition does not automatically mean a lack of harmony and balance. The example I usually give is that of a low energy, passive soul who might wish to combine with a restless, aggressive brain in order to combat the soul's natural inclination toward being tentative. On the other hand, if a powerful, self-indulgent soul with a tendency to control others is conjoined with an aggressive body, the mixture could prove to be volatile.

The identification of their true self through LBL therapy is not a guarantee that conflicting emotions and attitudes will be resolved by the client. Nevertheless, this therapy goes a long way in laying a more balanced psychological foundation of self-image through personal observation and self-reports. This should inspire greater perception and personal healing in your client's life. For you as the therapist, a major consideration of the LBL session is to explore the duality of egos within every hypnosis subject.

I have a case that illustrates a conflict of egos in opposition to one another. When I include this case in a training lecture my listeners tend to call it "The Case of the Dynamic Duo." The following excerpt is from a thirty-five-year-old unmarried woman, Lois, who is the sales manager for a large international company. Lois has a rather young soul, called Mawana, who has only been coming to Earth for around five hundred years. All this soul's previous lives have been as a man. Up until the current life, Mawana has always selected bodies on the basis of host compatibility. Now this has all changed. The scene I will describe occurred when I took my subject to the area of life selection just before her current life:

Dr. N: How many choices of host bodies are you given?

Mawana: Two: one is a man, the other a woman. I have the option of choosing another man like the ones I have had before. But I am going to take the woman because I must start expanding.

Dr. N: Well, Mawana, how does Lois look to you when you first see her?

Mawana: Ugh . . . skinny, high strung, hair all over the place . . . God, she is so . . . frantic. Oh, she is going to be a pistol to work with . . . I'm really setting myself up this time . . .

Dr. N: Meaning your past host bodies have not been so difficult in the melding, but this choice will be a change for your natural character?

Mawana: Yes. You see, I am a quiet, analytical soul. I carefully consider things before making a decision.

Dr. N: And why do you need a change?

Mawana: Because after examining all the possibilities of any situation I wind up not wanting to take any risks in my lives.

Dr. N: Are you telling me you have an indecisive soul?

Mawana: Oh . . . I don't think so . . . I'm just cautious.

Dr. N: And the body of Lois, what is her temperament like?

Mawana: A bomb ready to explode! She is off the wall . . . always initiating projects which lead to emotional quagmires.

Dr. N: Mawana, if this is the major area of contrast between your character and the temperament of your host body, what will you gain from this association that you did not have before in your other bodies?

Mawana: (long pause) It is hard for me to admit this, but I have been comfortable with emotionally cold hosts. It is so easy for me to be an observer and not fully commit to things . . . especially in my relationships. I have not been . . . open to people.

Dr. N: I see, and what has life been like for you in the body of Lois?

Mawana: A roller coaster ride! She is so . . . complicated . . . jumping into situations without much thought. Always ready to give all of herself to everything. I avoid anxiety; she does not. I am a plodder; she is self-motivating.

Dr. N: She expresses herself directly, where you are more indirect?

Mawana: That's putting it mildly. I try to slow her down but she is almost reckless . . . (tearfully) especially with men. Really, there are times when she is out of control and brings us so much emotional pain it is overwhelming.

Dr. N: And how does all this make you feel, Mawana?

Mawana: Trapped.

Note: I stop here for a while to comfort my client and get her back in focus on why she chose this body and how she can learn from it.

Dr. N: Tell me what the two of you have in common.

Mawana: (recovered) We are both caring in our own way. I'm more tentative about it. She brings out a warmth in my nature that I have found hard to express in the past. We both have intense pride and are not prone to anger or being vengeful with people who hurt us.

Dr. N: So that aspect of your ego duality has been rather harmonious?

Mawana: (somewhat reluctant) Mmm, yes . . . this part is an easier adjustment . . .

Dr. N: Okay, then, what is the one trait she has that you have most benefited from, Mawana?

Mawana: She is always ready to trust because she loves people. I am never bored and lonely as I was in my past lives. She pushes me.

Dr. N: And where do you help her the most?

Mawana: It has taken me a lot of time but finally I am getting her to slow down a little and think before she jumps.

We explored the differences between the bodies of men and women and I learned that Mawana, as a man, was rather self-centered and selfish with women. I think the change in direction by this soul, due in no small part to serious counseling between lives by her guide, was the result of being fed up with poor relationships due to a lack of bonding as a man. I believe our session together helped Lois and Mawana to see each other in a clearer light.

Lois has started to listen more to her inner self after a long series of emotionally destructive relationships. Months after the session, Lois wrote to me to explain that she is now more aware that both her egos are learning from each other and she is striving to bring balance into her "melded personality," as she calls it. Apparently, the two egos are achieving a symbiotic relationship at last.

When a person's behavior appears to have little or no connection to self, I think of an individual struggling to find their soul. One client told me, "I am a quiet soul with an affinity for open, accepting human minds. They are just easier for me during the joining." Another client had an opposing viewpoint: "I want resistance from an opposing brain right from the beginning because the work is more demanding and a greater challenge when we are not alike. Both of us will gain more from the association." There are no magic formulas in LBL work. Each case must be individually evaluated.

When I interact with a client about their body and soul duality, I ask myself three primary questions:

A. Is the intended goal of my client's soul-ego thwarted by different interests and motivations posed by their current body? What activities produce gratification as opposed to anxiety?
B. Is the duality of my client's soul-mind and body-mind pulling them in opposition or conjunction, and are either of these conditions intentional for progress?
C. Is my client socialized within his or her environment and human society or does this individual feel depersonalized, perhaps with thoughts that they do not belong on Earth?

Generally, souls have more resistance from some bodies than others in their long span of physical incarnations. To the spiritual regressionist working with disturbed clients in trance, it may appear that a struggle is going on with the soul trying to cope with the neurosis of a human organism. The spirit has the power to heal the body, while the body has the power to shut down the soul with primitive defense mechanisms. A primary goal of the LBL therapist is to assist clients in their search for internal harmony through greater comprehension about themselves and their origins. You want this self-assessment by the client to continue long after their session is over.

During my lectures I am often asked, "What about those souls inside physically disabled bodies? Why would anyone choose to live such confining and painful lives?" Some members of my audiences believe the souls who occupy crippled bodies were sent into them without prior knowledge because no other soul would want them. In my experience, this is not true. Souls volunteer for the really difficult lives and are encouraged in the life selection room to see what is in store for them. We are not sandbagged by guides. Souls know in advance about the specific karmic lessons they will face and how they would benefit from living a burdensome life.

I had a client who is a teacher for disabled children. One of her pupils is a wheelchair-bound boy by the name of Josh. This boy is so disabled he can hardly move or speak. She told me Josh "talks" with his eyes and facial expressions and has a wonderful smile. In deep hypnosis, my client saw Josh as a member of a more advanced soul group to which she also belongs. We learned that Josh has an aggressive, domineering, action-oriented soul with such powerful energy vibrations that he tends to override most of the quiet, introverted bodies he has chosen. Conversely, this soul sends extroverted, high-strung bodies out of control. She told me that it was mutually decided that the soul of Josh needed to experience a body which forced him to be still and contemplative. The assignment appears to be working.

Naturally, extroverted and introverted souls learn from all their associations with thousands of bodies during their incarnations. We are given the bodies we need to overcome major obstacles encountered in life. It has been said that we are never given more in life than we can handle, and to a large extent this seems to be accurate. We are who we are by design. There is a question I like to ask clients that can be very enlightening: Of all the bodies you have occupied, which one was your most favorite and why?

46

Therapeutic Benefits of Spiritual Regression

As an LBL hypnotherapist, your preferences may lean toward the Psychoanalytic, Behavioral, Gestalt, Insight-Oriented, or Free-Association approach, to name some therapies. Actually, I have seen a great diversity of philosophic orientation with my LBL students. Perhaps this is because many hypnosis practitioners are eclectic humanists. While this textbook reflects my own style, I believe there is no all-encompassing "right" way to practice LBL therapy. Many psychological approaches can be effectively integrated into spiritual regression. Occasionally a prospective client, particularly someone who has been exposed to more traditional psychotherapy, will ask about the psychological and clinical aspects of LBL hypnotherapy beyond what you would normally discuss during the intake interview.

I think in the beginning it is best to avoid long psychological explanations, even if you are inclined to do so, because this is not really what the client wants to know. I find what captures the attention of most clients is a brief discussion of hypnotherapy in general terms and its therapeutic use in uncovering the soul. I stress the importance of a harmony of energy between the soul-mind and human body. Whenever possible, keep things simple to avoid creating concerns, especially with a client who is anxious about any sort of intervention. It is wise to make it clear that while LBL hypnosis is a powerful tool for spiritual memory recall and conflict resolution, by itself it is not psychotherapy.

With some clients who press me further about therapy, I will say that regression into the unconscious mind to recover memories of past lives and the soul-state between those lives becomes curative when there is acquisition of greater insight into our true self. I tell the client this process allows for greater enlightenment of the conscious mind, particularly with the release of any stored negative energy. Frankly, I would prefer not to go into further detail in this area of therapy before the session because it could lead to misconceptions. I want the client to begin our work with an open mind. However, therapeutic revelations at the end of the session are another matter.

Once your client is in a superconscious state, they will know what is psychologically obstructing their potentialities far better than you imagined. As the session progresses, this self-awareness assumes even greater proportions. In my view, the difference between past life regression and spiritual regression is that LBL therapy allows for an easier transformation of perception. The client moves from seeing themselves in lives comprised of many temporary personalities to viewing a true version of self, emanating from one recognized immortal character in a spiritual setting.

As the spiritual regression session draws to a close, I want to know the following therapeutic information:

A. Is my client at a place in the session where they are able to identify their soul's desires and aspirations?
B. Are they able to make meaningful interpretations about the spiritual message they have received?
C. Within their script of life, do they have the capability of acting on their new awareness by restructuring negative imprints?

Despite having had prior psychotherapy, many clients will come to you with negative behavior patterns and poor attitudes.

Hypnosis regression enables therapists to more quickly assess the roots of emotional injuries. Yet trauma is not cured by just remembering the source. A client has to understand the meaning behind events and how all experiences affect the soul. Through LBL therapy, reducing the distortions and confusion arising out of current emotional dilemmas gives the client a chance to pull back a curtain, revealing their higher selves. This allows them to observe their whole personhood in a more objective light.

Working with clients in their soul-state is not just limited to visions of life between lives. With certain subjects, it is possible to use the duality of mind and spirit effectively in traumatic scenes involving the client's current incarnation to elicit information directly from their soul. This technique is similar to the three-way conversations I describe between facilitator, subject, and guides under case thirteen in Journey of Souls. Third-party communications can be just as effective between facilitator, subject, and the soul. The voice sounds of the client may change when they are talking through their own soul, just as it can when a guide is communicating through them.

In my own LBL, facilitated by a skillful and intuitive hypnotherapist, I was in a scene in my current life, at age seven, being dropped off at a boarding school. My soul seemed to be hovering over my body. Later, when I listened to my tape recording of this portion of the session, I realized I had been speaking in a different tone of voice as my soul objectively described the need for instilling courage and resolve into the mind of a little boy overcome by loneliness and the sadness of parental abandonment. The intensity of this therapeutic avenue is very revealing.

In my years of work, I found that when the client sees themselves as an immortal being in their mind's eye and discovers they are not just here by biological chance, they begin to address their inner truths. While appreciating the conflicts from their historical past, releasing them and reframing perceptions of who they really are moves them forward in life. Clients are more capable of coming to terms with their place in the scheme of things when they see their immortality. After an LBL session they know there is order and purpose and they have a part to play in this scheme. This insight allows for restructuring their model of the world and the management necessary to complete goals.

Although it is short term, I am not suggesting that LBL therapy is a quick fix for the client's problems. Former clients have written me years after their LBL sessions to explain they continue to process the information they acquired. Nevertheless, they have a better grasp of reality and their place in a perplexing world. They feel more focused and productive and aware of the hurt suffered by others.

Spiritual regression gives clients the realization that they are not alone, even if their life is solitary. This is because they are able to see their immortal connections to a community of soul companions who are, or were, in the bodies of relatives, lovers, friends, and acquaintances. To know for certain that you have value to others in the cosmos, regardless of your present surroundings in life, is very empowering. I recommend to my clients that they spend some quiet time each day getting in touch with the powers who watch over them. This is easier with their newfound knowledge and it fosters internal peace. Solitude, away from the everyday distractions, opens channels to an intuitive inner voice.

When I ask clients in a soul-state what they do in the spirit world to bring themselves into a keener state of awareness, they say they go into seclusion and focus on the pure state of their being. Of course this is easier for a discarnate because they are unencumbered by the sensory and emotional input of a physical body and all the material distractions of life. Even so, the concept is the same for an incarnated soul. One of the gains of reconnecting with the spirit world on a regular basis after an LBL session is contacting spirit guides.

We have seen the benefits in spiritual regression where clients become familiar with their personal spirit guides. When I work with a client in LBL therapy, I feel both the presence of my own guide and that of my client's guide monitoring me. There is no doubt in my mind that I am being assisted in uncovering psychological elements that may be inhibiting my client's progress. Never forget that it is your client's guide who is their primary therapist, not you. After the client leaves your office it is their master teacher whom they will turn to in future for solace. Spirit guides are the ultimate personal therapists.

Regardless of the intentions of each client and the frustrations you will encounter in this work, all clients must be treated with deference and understanding. I believe in challenging my clients but an LBL facilitator has to be careful during final therapeutic evaluations never to place the client on the defensive or cause them to feel threatened by the revelations you have helped them to uncover. Because the use of hypnotherapy in LBL work is such a powerful medium, it can subvert the practitioner into a personal power-trip.

Humility is the key to being an effective healer because you are being guided by a power greater than yourself. It is far more compelling to demonstrate nurturance and empathy rather than authority. This goes to the issue of your own self-concept, skill of expression, and experience. Spiritual regression involving the exposure of the soul embodies a sacred trust and we must honor it.

Part Six
CLOSING THE SESSION

47

Preparation for Embarkation

When the review of your client's last visit to the life selection area is completed, the end of the session is near. By way of review, chapter fourteen in Journey of Souls is devoted entirely to the soul's preparation for embarkation. In my training classes, students ask, "Do all souls prepare for a new life in the same way?" The answer is no, they don't. Not only are there differences in how souls get ready for their next incarnation, but the same souls prepare in different ways from one life to the next.

At this point in the session I would ask my client:

> I want you to explain what you are doing just before you leave the spirit world to incarnate into your current life.

There will be a variety of responses from clients, depending on the nature of the life to come and the level of advancement of the soul. The following is a short list of reasons behind differing client reactions:

A. Some clients will remember nothing about the final phase of incarnation preparations. They recall finishing with life selection and then being inside their mother's womb.

B. Some clients will talk about going to a preparation class for a final review of those aspects that are most important in the life to come. There are two variables here.
   1. They may meet only with guides.
   2. They may meet with guides and other souls who will be playing important roles in their lives.

C. Some souls will say a quick goodbye to a few friends in their soul group and immediately go to the place of embarkation in the company of their guide.
D. Some souls appear to be in solitude just before moving away from the spirit world. There are two variables here.
   1. They are unaware of a guide escorting them and suddenly find themselves in a fetus.
   2. They are escorted by a guide to the place of embarkation and experience the same sort of travel route into the fetus as most other souls.

I don't want to leave the reader with the impression that saying goodbye to soul group companions is ever short or nonexistent. It depends on when these farewells occur in the sequence of spiritual events. A quick au revoir just as the soul is ready to leave does not necessarily mean an absence of longer goodbyes at an earlier stage. Also, remember that a portion of our energy is not leaving the spirit world so it isn't as if our entire being is departing. What is left could be very active or inactive, depending how much we take with us, as I have mentioned under the topic of soul division. In either case, a soul's farewells to friends at some point can be intense, especially with those who will be incarnating with us into our next life.

The preparation or recognition classes designed for souls who are leaving the spirit world are often conducted by director-coordinators who are not the personal guides of the souls attending these classes. These directors, also known as prompters, are specialists in the dress rehearsals of meaningful scenes in the upcoming life. Essentially, they conduct the final reinforcement memory drills for departing souls. It is not unusual for the soul to be aware of companion and affiliated souls nearby who are slated to play important roles in the drama about to begin. The actual timing of birth in this new generation of children is apparently of no consequence for prep class attendance. As an example, you are five years older than your wife but both of you will attend the same prep class concerning your meeting each other.

There are clients who will describe their prep class as primarily oriented around the future recognition of soulmates. Others will tell you they experience reinforcement on one specific karmic lesson, and some will state their class had a combination of elements. When people feel déjà vu and synchronicity about certain events that they cannot explain in life, it is quite possible these sensations are reminders of their prep class.

There are many kinds of questions you might direct to your client at this phase of the session:
1. What triggers or red flags were you given in advance to help you remember the importance of certain events?
2. Can you tell me how you were supposed to remember significant people in your life?
3. What is the most meaningful aspect of your last prep class?

In rare instances you might hear a client exclaim that in the moments before embarkation into a new life they needed a little more persuasion or confidence-building by their guide. While these trepidations are very uncommon, no soul is forced to reincarnate if they want to back out at any time. I have already mentioned that only rarely have I encountered a soul who asked for a replacement once they were in the fetus. The majority of your clients will state that rather than being anxious, they were filled with joy, hope, and expectations about the life ahead. The percentage of my clients in this category was over 80 percent. Since a small percentage of clients do express some trepidations, I would recommend you consider asking the following questions in some form about client attitudes toward rebirth:
1. What were your primary reasons for coming this time around?
2. Did you sense it was your duty to come, as if a new incarnation was inevitable, or could you have stayed behind?

3. Would you characterize your attitude toward rebirth as being:
   a. Joyful and full of anticipation about opportunity for a new incarnation?
   b. One of indifference about another life?
   c. Cautious or reluctant about rebirth?

I have given a descriptive case example of the actual return to Earth by the soul under chapter fifteen, case twenty-nine, in Journey of Souls. If your client is able to describe this procedure, they will often say their guides accompany them a little way to a kind of exit portal before separating. The soul then has the sense they are passing down through some sort of vortex or tunnel back to Earth. In many cases the client will only vaguely remember the last stage of rebirth. They will remark, "I went from light into darkness (the portal) and then I felt warmth (in the womb)."

48

Completing the Spiritual Regression

After your analysis of the client's preparations for embarkation are completed, it is time to wrap up all the loose ends of the session. I often ask open-ended questions at this stage such as, "Well, how do you feel about all that you have learned?" You will find that, after experiencing the meaning of life through spiritual regression, clients are often struck by how seriously they have taken themselves over matters of no great concern. Seeing the larger purpose behind all their experiences gives the client greater perspective. After their sessions, clients write to me explaining that they are now addressing the more significant aspects of their lives with greater focus.

After viewing their spiritual existence between lives, decisions which lie ahead for the remainder of this life fill most clients with a new resolve. They know their body is a precious gift that they helped to choose. They see life as an opportunity for learning and enrichment and feel a greater confidence in themselves. Above all they realize that their reality has order and purpose.

By now both you and your client are very tired at the end of a session that has lasted over three hours. At some point near the end I always ask a catch-all question:

> Before we close and leave the spirit world, I want you to take a last look around and tell me if there is anything we might have missed of significance that you would like to discuss.

Most clients say no. Perhaps this is because they are as worn out as I am! However, once in a while, something in their mind crops up, such as an activity we missed or one specific issue that needs to be clarified. By the time the session is over, most clients believe they have recovered those memories that were intended for them.

49

Awakening the LBL Client

Your LBL client must be brought out of their deep trance state with much care. After such a long period of hypnosis, the major part being in a superconscious Theta state, your subject is going to feel a great heaviness and even numbness of the body. They might also be a little disoriented for a few minutes. This is because each person experiences an ego transformation from full soul engagement back into their current personality. For this reason, awakening must be handled slowly and with care.

Just because you have brought them out of trance does not mean clients immediately shed the vestiges of their soul connection. Indeed, for the rest of their lives, the client will retain a stronger internal connection with their soul. As they awaken, the client comes from a very safe place—the sanctuary of their permanent home—back into the hectic and demanding physical environment of planet Earth. Therefore, this transition must not be abrupt.

I would like to offer an example of how I start my awakening instructions at the end of spiritual regression:

> As we begin now to leave the high realm of your soul-mind and the beautiful existence in the spirit world between your lives on Earth, I want you to remember this loving world is always with you. Everything we have talked about—all your thoughts, your memories, and your insights—will be retained to help and empower

you as you complete the remainder of your current life with renewed energy and purpose. Allow this all-knowing knowledge to settle calmly within your conscious mind in proper perspective. Allow yourself to now feel completely whole as a single person that is you. Your immortal self is completely joined with your human self as a single unit as we now return back—higher and higher—back through the tunnel of time, into the present.

Certainly this mantra could be considered a post-hypnotic suggestion for the client but I use it for transition to an awake state. As a general rule, I do not believe that the traditional use of post-hypnotic suggestions are a necessary component of spiritual regression, particularly since you are sending the client home with tapes of their session. Posthypnotic suggestions can last for some time but I feel that spiritual regression has an enduring quality all by itself. From my experience, the assimilation of all memories recalled from the soul-mind about the spirit world will be retained by the client without formalized post-hypnotic suggestions.

All the studies of post-hypnotic suggestion indicate that when it is used, information which is especially relevant and meaningful will have greater durability. I have previously mentioned under the subject of guides that you might state, "You will never forget the images and exchanges with your personal spirit guide." The use of post-hypnotic suggestions might be appropriate in other specific areas, such as reinforcing any desensitization you performed for past life trauma.

Also, I don't rule out the possibility that designated memory reinforcements may be necessary with certain clients involving the council chamber, or a particular soul, to promote healing. These are judgement calls based upon each client and their session. I would not recommend that you attempt to breach any client blocks of amnesia about the spirit world, or the client's future destiny, through the use of post-hypnotic suggestions.

All hypnosis facilitators have their own methods for returning clients to a full awake state. What I have offered are my own preparations before the usual final awake instructions, where I will begin a numbers countdown. During this time I will ask for very deep breaths, including the customary commands for eye focus and clear-headedness, while I call for increased circulation and encourage clients to feel relaxed, happy, and fully refreshed.

50

The Exit Interview

After your client awakes from their spiritual experience, many will stare off into space for a few minutes in awe of what they have seen. Some will be tearful, while others will laugh for joy. Most feel the weight of expectations their spiritual masters have for them. I try to say very little at first because I want to give my client this quiet time for reflection. I will encourage them to just sit still and recover while I hand them a glass of water and prepare their tape recordings.

You will have two types of client responses to an LBL session. There are some who do not want to talk much about what they have seen because it is so private and personal they wish to collect their own thoughts in the days ahead without input from you. Often they will contact you later. A majority of clients, however, will immediately want to process the highlights of their session. In the beginning I would advise letting them lead the conversation in whatever direction they wish. They are overwhelmed with self-discovery. On a conscious level, they now realize the floodgate has been opened to their inner selves. While feeling excitement, they also have the sense of divine responsibility for their lives. This intensely personal validation of their identity brings authenticity to the client and their place in the world.

It is important to realize that many clients will solicit advice from you about the meaning of their sessions, and this is something you should be cautious about. Our task is to assist clients in finding their own interpretations to visualizations from the spirit world. Clients have a tendency to want direction and to have you help them with interpretations. Naturally, you can offer opinions regarding their life in the spirit world, but I would be careful about commenting on their future decision-making based on this information.

A good idea is to ask them general questions such as:
1. What did you gain most from your session?
2. How do you understand yourself better as a result of what you have learned?
3. In what way do you now have a greater comprehension of life and your place in it?
4. What possibilities and alternatives do you see that are opened to you now that you have this information?

Your client may not be able to address any of these sorts of questions right after their session with you. Spiritual regression is intended to give the client greater direction and purpose, but how they choose to do this is up to them. They may need a great deal of time for self-evaluation.

One of the advantages of the exit interview is to allow the client to become fully conscious from a long hypnosis session. This can take at least a half hour. You don't want them to rush out and jump into an automobile until they are fully focused. This is why I watch my client's eyes and body-motor movements carefully. While the subject is recovering from deep hypnosis, I explain that in the days and weeks ahead more bits and pieces from their released soul memories may continue to surface in flashbacks and dreams. I urge them to keep a diary or journal handy for jotting down spontaneous notes to build upon the data contained on their audio tapes. This brings up the issue of repeat LBL visits.

Since no single session will ever contain all the information people would like to have about their existence, it is natural for some clients to talk about returning a second time. They may request this on the spot but it is more likely they have gone home, listened to their tapes, reflected further on certain parts of the LBL session, and decided they want to see you again to learn more. It is my recommendation that, in all fairness, you should warn clients before they leave your office that they may not be able to recall anything more of substance with further sessions.

The reasons why a second LBL session would not be fruitful range from the client's capacity, inclinations of their guide, lessons to be learned, their stage of development, and so on. On the other hand, there is no question that a repeat session could bring out more substantial information with certain clients about their spiritual life. There is no prescribed approach to repeat sessions. Those subjects who had to work especially hard in hypnosis to access the spirit world are the ones you would want to take back through the childhood-past life-spirit world route. With other post-LBL clients you can avoid childhood regression and just work with induction, deepening, and a past life.

The deepening may not take as long the second time, especially if you have given your client a post-hypnotic suggestion from the initial session that any future regression sessions with you will go quickly and easily. You should use another past life in repeat sessions to gain natural entry into the spirit world. The past life should be a different one than before to give the client additional variety and detail. You will both learn more about the self-actualization of the subject's soul in different bodies with repeat sessions.

51

Conclusions

Many clients leave my office clutching their tapes as if they were gold and I wonder how they are going to apply what they have learned to give their lives new direction. I always feel that I could have probed for more information, helped them in better ways, and done more to bring them a greater awareness of all the wonders of their spiritual life. Every session is unique and whenever I am able to assist a client in unlocking their hidden knowledge about an immortal existence, I feel privileged.

When I started so many years ago I had to break new ground about the use of hypnosis to reach our life between lives, which you will not have to do. At the same time I know that future spiritual regressionists will carry this work far beyond what I have done. LBL hypnotherapy carries a great responsibility to give as much of yourself as you can because the sensibilities of each client are so complex.

In discovering their immortality, LBL clients see an unbroken life of succession in their existence. This gives them an understanding of their place in the continuity of life, death, and rebirth. Despite their current circumstances, people will leave your office knowing they have a permanent home in the afterlife—a place of love, peace, and forgiveness with highly advanced beings who care about them.

You will have clients who will ask that now they have gained all this information about themselves, what are they going to do with it? They are concerned about meeting the lofty goals that brought them into this life. I try to reassure them that our masters have infinite patience with us. I tell the departing client that we are measured not so much by what we do for ourselves but by how we have helped others along the way. I explain that in each lifetime we may falter, make mistakes, take the wrong paths, and make poor choices, but with every opportunity and decision we grow. The mark of a distinctive life is having the courage to keep picking ourselves up after setbacks and finishing our lives strong.

Appendix

The Way of Souls: Spiritual Principles

1. The soul cannot be defined or measured because it has no limits that are perceived about its divine creation. The most consistent reports of the soul's demonstrated essence is that it represents intelligent energy that is immortal and manifested by specific vibrational waves of light and color.
2. All human beings have one soul that remains attached to its chosen physical body until death. Souls do play a part in the selection of their next physical body during cycles of reincarnation. The soul typically joins its physical body after conception, between the fourth month and birth.
3. Each soul has a unique immortal character. When conjoined with a human brain, this ego character is melded with the emotional temperament, or human ego, of that body to produce a single but temporary personality for one lifetime. This is what is meant by the duality of our mind.
4. While soul memory may be hidden from the level of conscious awareness through amnesia, thought patterns of the soul influence the human brain to induce motivations for certain actions.
5. Souls reincarnate with human beings for countless lifetimes to advance through levels of development by addressing karmic tasks from former lifetimes. Each personality in every life contributes to the evolution of the soul. Souls grow in knowledge and wisdom through this learning process while pondering their thoughts and deeds in past lives under the direction of their spiritual teachers between lives.
6. Our planet is one of an incalculable number of worlds that serve as training schools for the advancement of souls. During temporary physical incarnations on Earth, souls are

provided an opportunity to advance through trial and error to accumulate wisdom. Humans are not bound to a predetermined existence. Various possibilities and probabilities arising from karmic influences and prior soul contracts are subject to the free will of the soul.

7. Earth is a place of great beauty and joy but also harbors ignorance, hate, and suffering that are man-made combined with natural planetary disasters over which we have little control. Coping with these positive and negative elements on Earth is by design. This planet is a testing ground for souls rather than being a place of evil, demonic influence from outside our world. Spiritual malevolence does not exist within the divine order of love and compassion that comprises our spiritual origins.

8. Personal enlightenment emanates from within each of us and endows humans with the capability to reach our own divine power without intermediaries.

9. At the moment of physical death the soul returns to the spirit world and the source of its creation. Since a portion of a soul's energy has never left the spirit world during incarnation, the returning soul rejoins with that essence of itself. Thus, spiritual learning never ceases for the soul. The spirit world also offers souls the opportunity for rest and reflection between physical lives.

10. Souls appear to be members of specific spirit cluster groups to whom they have been assigned since their creation. The teachers of each group are the personal spirit guide of members of that group. Spiritual companions of these groups reincarnate with the soul and assume meaningful roles in the drama of a soul's life on Earth.

11. Rather than being defined as a place of ultimate inaction, or nirvana, the spirit world appears to be a space of transition for souls who evolve into higher energy forms with capabilities for creation of animate and inanimate objects. The soul's energy itself has been created by a higher source.

The spirit world has an area of influence that is undefined except that it appears to include our universe and nearby dimensions.
12. No earthly religious deities are seen in the spirit world by returning souls. A soul's closest connection to a divine power is with their personal spirit guide and members of a council of benevolent counselors who monitor the affairs of each soul. Souls from Earth feel and sense the presence of a godlike Oversoul or Source emanating from above the wise beings who make up individual councils.
13. The spirit world seems to be directed by highly advanced non-reincarnating soul specialists who regulate the work of the souls in their care. When incarnating souls develop to higher levels of wisdom and performance themselves, they will cease to incarnate and take their place among these specialists, who will assist the still-incarnating souls. Soul specialists apparently are selected by motivation, talent, and performance.
14. The ultimate goal of all souls appears to be the desire to seek and find perfection, and finally conjoin with the Source who created them.

ILLUSTRATIONS

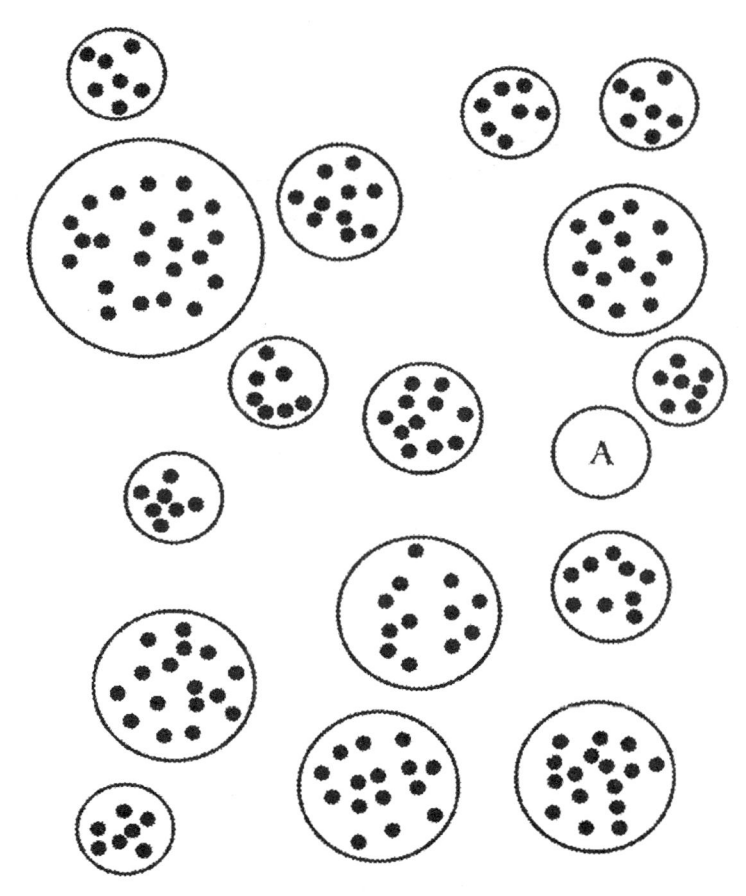

Figure 1: The Great Hall Community Center. This diagram represents the first view by many people of large numbers of primary soul cluster groups that make up one big secondary group of some 1,000 souls. Primary group A is the subject's own cluster of souls.

Appendix | 215

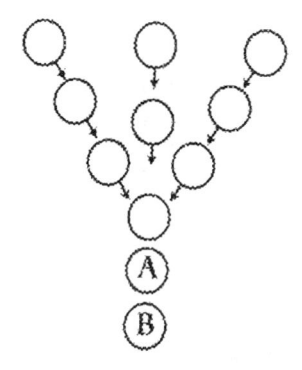

Figure 2: Indicates the phalanx-diamond position of a primary cluster group greeting returning soul A with the group guide B behind. Here many souls are concealed behind one another before their turn to greet the incoming member.

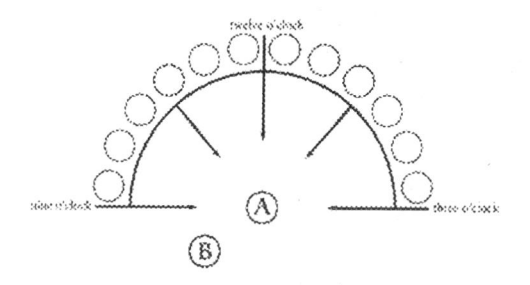

Figure 3: Indicates the more common semi-circle positioning of a soul group waiting to greet returning soul A with (or without) the guide teacher in position B. On the hands of this clock diagram, souls come forward, each in their own turn, from positions within a 180-degree are. Typically, greeting souls do not come from behind A in the six O'clock position.

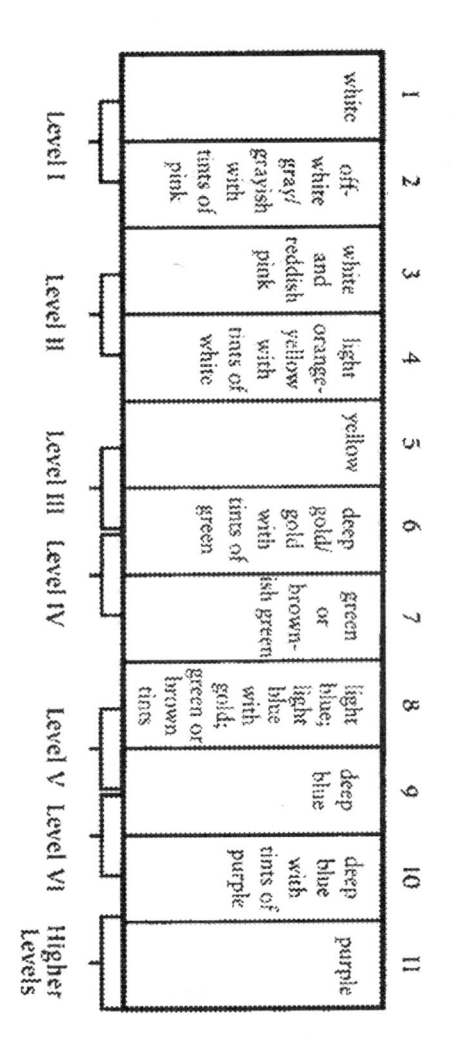

Level	Box	Color
Level I	1	white
Level I	2	off-white grayish with tints of pink
Level II	3	white and reddish pink
Level II	4	light orange-yellow with tints of white
Level III	5	yellow
Level III	6	deep gold/gold with tints of green
Level IV	7	green or brownish green
Level V	8	light blue; light blue with green or brown gold; tints
Level V	9	deep blue
Level VI	10	deep blue with tints of purple
Higher Levels	11	purple

Figure 4: Color Spectrum of Spiritual Auras. This classification chart indicates how a soul's primary core colors deepen from beginners in box 1 to ascended masters in box 11. Halo-color overlaps of different hues may surround the primary core colors of a soul. There is also an overlapping of color aura between soul Level 1 to VI.

Appendix | 217

Primary Core Colors

2	3	4	5
off-white	white-pinkish	orange-yellow	yellow

Secondary Halo Colors

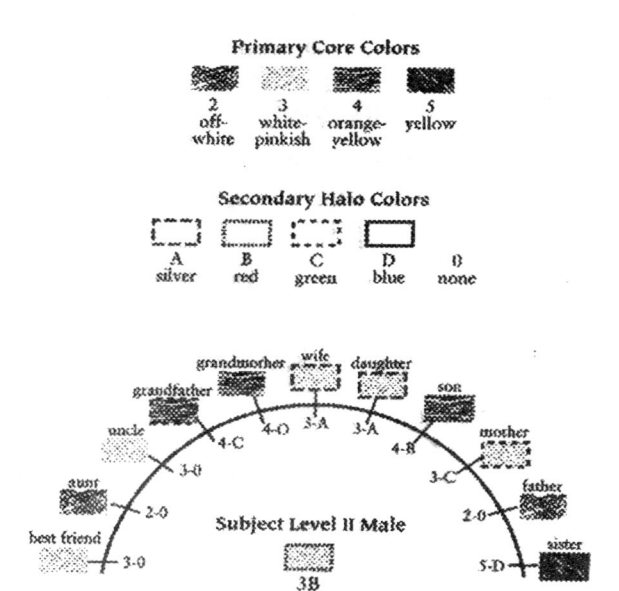

A	B	C	D	0
silver	red	green	blue	none

Subject Level II Male

Figure 5: Energy Colors Displayed by a Soul Group. This chart indicates the currently incarnated relatives and one friend of subject 3B. The boxes for each relative are keyed to figure 4 for both core and halo colors. Numbered boxes 2, 3, 4, and 5 are primary core colors. Lettered boxes A, B, C, and D are secondary halo colors displayed by group members.

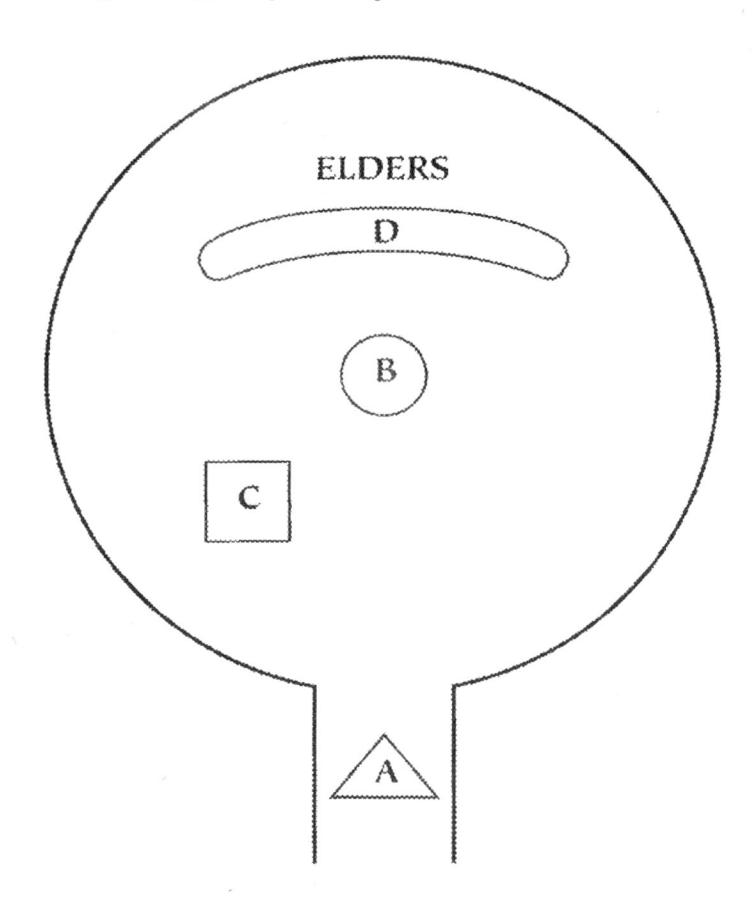

Figure 6: The Council Chamber. A typical structural design where Elders meet souls. This spacious room appears to most people as a large rotunda with a dome ceiling. Souls enter the chamber at the end of hallway A, or from an alcove. The soul is positioned in the center B, with their guide in back, usually on the left C. The Elders generally sit at a long crescent-shaped table D, in front of the soul. The table may appear to be rectangular.

Index

aborted sessions, 89
affiliated souls, 136, 161
Alpha state, 20
amnesia, 120, 179, 235
appointment, 3, 29
Atlantis attraction, 65, 66, 187
attachment and releasement, 79
attendance, 30, 64, 170, 195
audio cassette tapes, 86
auditory, 44, 83
awakening, 85
Beta state, 20, 39
bias, 4, 6, 24, 187
blocking, 89, 90, 91, 92
body imprints, 189
body selection, 56, 168, 183
brain waves, 156
burn-out, 17
character, 142, 157, 160, 161, 185
chi (Taoism), 13
childhood trauma, 33
children souls, 163
choices, v, 14, 98, 102, 108
clock technique, 138
colonization, 187
colors
    blue, 24, 67, 109, 110, 142, 143
    gold, 142, 233
    green, 142, 172
    purple, 142, 143, 172
    red, 223
    silver, 142, 173
    white, 44, 45, 62, 109, 110, 122, 163
    yellow, 109, 139, 142
colors (core and halo), 109, 142
colors (meaning), 45, 109, 141, 143
colors (spiritual auras), 141, 143, 159
companion souls, 127, 135, 149, 158
Confidentiality, 31
conscious interference, 39, 54, 65, 67, 69
conscious mind, 5, 13, 27, 31, 39, 67, 148, 228
contacting loved ones, 84
contaminated Souls, 120, 206
council visits, 166, 191
crosschecking, 67
crystals, 119
dark souls, 79, 142
dates (past lives), 68
death scenes, 60, 73, 189
déjà vu, 223
Delta state, 21
Destiny of Souls, 80, 84, 109, 110, 111, 114, 120
determinism, 200
directors (spiritual)
    council, 79, 124, 157
    life selection room, 197, 199, 201, 202, 212
    preparation class, 43, 52
disabled bodies, 212
disengagement, 51
disoriented client, 79, 85, 166
dissatisfaction, 4, 28
division, 39, 114, 153, 155
duality, 10, 90, 207, 208, 210, 211, 235
ego (duality) See body versus soul, 69, 90, 181, 206, 210
energy fields, 47, 57

energy restoration, 110, 114, 116, 118, 119, 120
envelopment, 110
Ericksonian methods, 44
fallibility (souls), 22
Famous Person Syndrome, 66
fantasy, 25, 27, 90
fetus, 55, 57, 61, 204, 222, 223
figure reference (illustrations)
  diamond positions, 239
figure references (illustrations)
  half-circle position, 137
  recreation halls, 134
first past life, 186, 187
flashbacks, 231
focus effect, 14
fogging, 86
fractionation, 43
free will, 6, 148, 183, 199, 200, 236
future. See hypnosis progression, 89
gender, 68, 122, 171, 186
geography, 10, 68
guide recognition, 112, 114, 138, 222
homecoming, 113, 114, 166
hunkering-down syndrome, 152
hybrid souls, 25, 66, 187, 188
hypnosis
  authoritarian, 11, 37, 44, 160
  awakening, 227
  deepening, 21, 32, 37, 40, 41, 43, 44, 48, 91, 232
  defensive reactions, 43
  desensitization, 73, 78, 228
  directive guidance, 85
  free association, 19, 136, 161
  hand movements, 231
  ideomotor signal, 53, 66
  indirect suggestion, 21, 44
  induction approach, 37, 48, 232
  memory recall, 41, 54, 215
  memory reinforcement, 229
  permissive, 11, 37, 44
  post-hypnotic suggestions, 228, 229
  prior exposure, 13, 19, 28, 61, 218
  progression, 6, 16, 125, 183, 184
  pyramiding, 38, 43
  receptivity, 11, 17, 37, 40, 41
  recovery, 20, 120
  resistance, 62, 90, 101, 107
  revivification, 41
  self-sabotage, 19, 94
  somnambulistic, 41
  susceptibility, 23, 80, 180
  techniques, 48, 61, 80, 94
  trance depth, 20, 21, 42, 51, 54, 55, 69
  validity, 67, 69
identification, 136, 138, 147, 152, 157, 186, 208
incarnated energy, 154, 155, 156
independent study group, 118, 163, 164
inner circle, 151, 152, 157
interdimensional travel, 142, 192
intuition, 11, 123, 207
Journey of Souls, ii, v, xi, 106, 121
junior guides, 121
karma, 75, 142, 150
kinesthetic, 44, 83
library, 82, 103, 118, 127, 166
lost loves, 210
luminosity, 110, 144
mapping, 10, 16
medallions, 172
metaphoric, 15, 44, 94

Multiple Personality Disorder, 205
names, 29, 115, 140
Near Death Experience, 25
now time, 80, 182, 199, 200
observer versus participant, 73, 86, 177
orientation, 79, 116, 118, 120, 122, 123
pacing, 48, 137
parallel lives, 154
past life, v, xi, xii, 13, 16, 18
permeation, 110
personality, 27, 44, 90, 91, 133
possession theory, 125, 204
post-hypnotic suggestions, 22, 111, 232
prana, 14
preconceptions, 5, 24, 69, 121
prep class, 223
presence, 102, 180, 218, 237
primary groups, 164
Principle of Self, 206
privacy, 31, 95, 96
pseudo-recall, 18
psychodrama, 160, 192, 193, 194
purpose, 27, 29, 74, 97, 149, 217, 225, 231
Quantum Theory, 200
questions, xi, 20
rebirth, 168, 223, 224, 233
re-entry variables (souls), 193, 198
reframing, 59, 74, 217
reincarnation, 5, 16, 154, 235
religious influence, 3, 190
remodeling, 120
repeat LBL, 231
Samskaras (negative karma), 190

secondary groups (affiliated), 133, 136
sentient (subjects), 62, 83
sequencing, 222
sessions, xii, 3, 4, 17, 19, 26, 98, 152, 225, 232
solitude, 118, 119, 127, 222
soulmates, 24, 60, 133, 136, 147, 223
sound, 38, 48, 113, 115
spirit guide, 69, 77, 97, 101, 103, 107, 115, 218, 228, 237
student teachers, 163
subconscious, 16, 39, 90, 101
symbolic, 14, 44, 94, 114, 124, 133, 169
synchronicity, 132, 181
telepathic, 14, 113, 179
therapeutic approches, 75, 120
Theta state, 20, 37, 40, 227
third party technique, 122
time
    distortion (linear), 46
    distortion (realities), 216
    now, v, 6, 10
    shifting, 11
    suspension, 182
    timelines (causality), 103
    timelines (future events), 182
    timelines (multiple causality), 86
    timelines (pasr events), 198
vibrational energy (soul), 48, 110
visualization
    classroom, 118, 158, 159, 166, 193
    community halls, 133, 134
    council chamber, 170, 229
    countryside, 63, 85, 132, 133
    gardens, 134

libraries, 132, 134
life selection, 56, 102, 169, 177, 182, 183, 191, 198, 200, 201
soul group, 133, 134, 135, 137, 141, 147, 161, 193
temples, 132
visualization instruction (listed in order of usage)
breathing, 46
childhood images, 33, 52
disengagement, 46
regression preparations, 19
visulization
council chambers, 169
voice, 77, 102, 170, 195, 216, 217
walk-in theory, 204
womb, 33, 54, 55, 56